PSYCHOLOGICAL NEEDS
AND CULTURAL SYSTEMS

A Case Study

by
JOEL ARONOFF
Michigan State University

AN INSIGHT BOOK

D. VAN NOSTRAND COMPANY, INC.
PRINCETON, NEW JERSEY
TORONTO   LONDON

Van Nostrand Regional Offices:
New York, Chicago, San Francisco

D. Van Nostrand Company, Ltd., London

D. Van Nostrand Company (Canada), Ltd., Toronto

PRINTED IN THE UNITED STATES OF AMERICA

To
ROBERT L. BRADSHAW

Preface

Although the field of Culture and Personality has offered the promise of forming the link between the social sciences, it has become apparent that we have not yet worked out a conceptual framework to integrate these areas in a meaningful way. One need only examine the various Culture and Personality readers to feel the pristine isolation in which each topic is held. Yet, what is also clear, is the implicit conception in both Psychology and Anthropology that personalty is mainly a function of the social system. This lingering heritage of a now rejected cultural relativism attempts to solve the problem of relating the separate psychological and social systems by treating psychological processes as the resultants of social determinants: essentially presenting personality as an epiphenomenon.

It is my belief that a fruitful approach to the creation of a general theory may lie in taking seriously the claims that certain psychological drives are basic to the human organism, and discovering their links to processes on the sociological level. In this book I have attempted to explore this problem, suggest a basis for the integration of psychological and sociological processes, and test out the model through an empirical field study of two subcultures in a West Indian village. From this perspective, I believe, it can be demonstrated that the organization of both social and psychological systems is the final product of three independent factors: environment, institutional determinants, and organismically based psychological needs. I will try to show that they have a strong reciprocal influence on one another, and that to understand the dynamics of either system one must discover the means and degree of their interaction.

The village of Dieppe Bay on the island of St. Kitts in

the British West Indies served as the laboratory for testing the hypothesis. On the basis of a preliminary field trip, the economic work group and family organizations of fishermen and cane cutters were chosen for special study. Using a combination of techniques, including intensive field observation, formal interviewing, and projective tests to isolate the separate factors, the significant differences found in the structures of these organizations were analyzed and traced back to the determinants proposed in the theoretical model. In this way it was possible to confront directly the prevailing reliance on economic or social determinants, as well as to break out of the circular problem of separating what seem to be isomorphic social and psychological processes. In the social sciences, the controversy over the relative importance of social versus psychological processes has been of long duration. By attempting to maintain a constant interchange between the empirical and theoretical dimensions of this study, it was hoped to argue the case in the scientific arena of evidence, rather than with the tools of polemic.

JOEL ARONOFF

Acknowledgments

I should like to thank the people of Dieppe Bay, whose generous hospitality and understanding toward a stranger contributed to a pleasurable experience that went far beyond the bounds of the field work, itself. Although this list might be endlessly extended, I must thank especially my friends, Mr. Richard Martin, Mr. Joseph 'Son' Martin, Mrs. Albertha Matthew, Miss Marilyn Tweede, Mr. James Brown, and Mr. Livingstone James, who came to feel that this work was their own. I am also deeply grateful to the Honorable Robert L. Bradshaw and to Mr. George Warren, both of whom, though seeing the problems of St. Kitts from radically different perspectives, contributed immeasurably to my understanding of the island. I am also indebted to Mr. Joseph Williams, to Mr. William Herbert, and to Dr. Sebastian and Dr. Lake.

To Arthur Warmoth, I should like to express my thanks for being a five-year discussant on the problems of psychology and for his time and patience in scoring the projective test. I am also grateful to Nathaniel Raymond, who did field work in a neighboring village on St. Kitts, for our many discussions. Much of what I know of the art of field work I learned from him.

My wife, Marilyn Aronoff, herself an anthropologist, participated in all phases of the field work. Her sensitivity, insight and skill enriched every aspect of this study.

I should like to express my appreciation to Dr. Eugenia Hanfmann and Dr. Kurt Wolff who read this manuscript with careful attention and made many helpful suggestions. I benefited greatly from numerous conversations with Dr. Mark Spivak, whose unfailing generosity and keen criticism clarified innumerable difficulties.

I am especially indebted to three men. In Dr. David

Aberle I found an anthropologist whose criticisms helped me to formulate what I really wanted to do. His incisive presentation of the contemporary anthropological point of view, and his methodological and theoretical comments, have pursued me throughout my research. My gratitude, of course, does not obligate him to the views expressed in this work. Dr. Ulric Neisser provided a source of constant encouragement, evaluation, and advice in every step of my research. His early suggestions helped bring an amorphous research problem into focus while the many hours we have spent working together on the analysis of the data have been, for me, an experience of great meaning and pleasure. Finally, I am deeply grateful for the opportunity to have studied with Dr. Abraham Maslow, whose theories of personality have provided such a rich source of ideas, and whose teaching embodies his vision of what psychology might be.

The research carried out on St. Kitts was made possible by a Pre-Doctoral Fellowship #MH-13,721-04 from the National Institute of Mental Health. I am very grateful for their continued support. My thanks also go to the Research Institute for the Study of Man and its Director, Dr. Vera Rubin, for supplementary travel funds and for access to the invaluable research facilities of the Institute.

To Mrs. Elizabeth Griffin, who was responsible for the preparation of this manuscript, I wish to express my appreciation for her care and skill, and for the pleasure of her company.

J.A.

Contents

List of Tables

I

The Need for an Integrated
Theory of Culture and Personality

The disciplines of social science, traditionally, lay claim to somewhat isolated bodies of theory and data. Integrating the discoveries of these separate fields presents great difficulty, as each discipline tends to organize all phenomena in terms of its own central conceptions or else defers prematurely to the authority of another. In the interest of establishing a conceptual framework which would genuinely integrate the discoveries of these fields, I should like to open, once again, the issue of the relationship between basic psychological needs and cultural institutions.

In the field of Personality and Culture, which has emerged as the meeting ground for interdisciplinary research and theory, the main focus of contemporary formulations has been placed on the cultural determinants of personality. Thus, it has been assumed that cultural forms can be analyzed only in cultural terms, and personality structure is primarily dependent upon the requirements of the cultural system. Since this conclusion draws back from an examination of organismically-based psychological drives and the possibility of their influence on the cultural system, it is essential to develop a conceptual framework capable of handling all these issues and to reveal the significance of all of the determinants that may together structure the organization of the social field. This book will attempt to demonstrate that although psychological and sociocultural systems are distinct levels of the social field, they strongly influence each other. The proper understanding of the dynamics of either system depends upon the discovery of the means and degree of their interaction.

In view of the present trend to seek explanations of

1

cultural phenomena primarily in environmental or social forces, the issue with which this research most particularly deals is the selective nature of the human being. The question may be posed quite simply. Is the individual no more than a neutral carrier of culture, who accepts the motives needed to maintain his particular society, or does he have basic needs which the culture is, in part, organized to gratify?

Although much evidence has been gathered to show that the human being is extraordinarily adaptable and can be shaped in many extreme ways by the cultural environment in which he is found, yet he is not infinitely malleable. Within the diversity of motivations, basic drives have been found which underlie all of his patterns of action. When these drives are frustrated, he continues to search for some channel of gratification. From the genetic timetables of Freud, to Jung's notion of compensation, to the various need theories of contemporary psychologists like Erikson and Maslow, great emphasis has been placed on the innate tendencies which bring the individual into a relationship with the environment and determine the course of his actions.[1] Because psychological needs of this kind have been neglected in studies of social phenomena, it is essential to investigate the possibility that they may interact with environmental and social determinants to form a particular culture.

One aim of this study will be to make explicit some of the needs which may be influential in forming the sociocultural system. In the theorizing of most anthropologists, even those completely committed to explanations on the environmental or cultural level, there is usually an implicit conception of personality. Their views often suggest that personality is a residue of acquired motivation and thus is of no importance in culture-formation. (For an example of this trend, see the discussion of Dorothy Lee, below.) Such theories may frequently rest on as vague a concept as "positive affect," as if there

[1] There are many other psychologists who have contributed to our knowledge of organismically-based needs. Among those whose works support this position are McDougall (1960), Goldstein (1939), Adler (1956), White (1963), and Angyal (1941).

could be positive affect without a drive which is being affected positively. Yet even to say that the individual can be shaped by the requirements of culture and has no particular needs that must be gratified is to hold a theory of human personality which is not consonant with the findings of many contemporary psychologists.

On the other hand, anthropologists often revert to single, isolated psychological needs when their purely cultural argument gets sticky. Many fragmentary theories of human nature are found in the work of those who firmly deny the individual a causative role. An example may be found in the writings of Julian Steward who states: "Personality is shaped by culture, but it has never been shown that culture is affected by personality" (1958, p. 7). However, when he requires an explanation for patriliny he appeals to a principle of "innate male dominance" (p. 125). In either case, whether the human being is seen merely as a "carrier," or whether an innate principle is asserted to fit the need of a particular argument, some theory of human nature has been assumed.[2] Since we cannot avoid making assumptions about human needs, it is best to bring them explicitly and firmly into the attempt at causal explanation.

One clear reason for the anthropologists' flight from basic human needs is the failure of psychology to provide a secure determination of the human drive system. Historically, lists of needs have only generated counterlists, while their proponents argued over their composition until the entire venture was shelved. As a result, most psychologists have refused to take seriously the conflicting claims of the various lists. It is not unreasonable, therefore, that anthropologists should conclude with Dorothy Lee (1959) that:

> The concept of an inventory of basic needs rose to fill the vacuum created when the behaviorists banished the old list of instincts. . . . When we found that the original list of basic needs or drives was inadequate, we, like the psychologists, tried to solve the difficulty by adding on a list of social and psychic needs. . . . When the list proved faulty, all we had to do was add to the list. . . .

[2] Wallace (1962) makes a similar point in an analysis of a passage of Radcliff-Brown.

I am not saying here that there are no needs; rather, that if there are needs, then they are derivative rather than basic . . . I believe that it is value, not a series of needs, which is at the bases of human behavior. [And] It is possible to see needs as arising out of the basic values of a culture. . . .

We create needs in the infant by withholding affection and then presenting it [affection] as a series of approvals for an inventory of achievements or attributes. . . . And thus, through habituation and teaching, the mother reproduces in the child her own needs.

When we look closely at Lee's phrasing, we find that socially determined needs rest on such psychological causes as the withholding of affection from infants. Although Lee has avoided the use of the word "need," in her attempt to demonstrate that "Culture is a system which stems from and expresses . . . the basic values of the society," it is clear that she, like Steward, found it necessary to base her account of culture on the social development of an innate psychological force. The proper response, of course, to the problem of identifying needs in an accurate and meaningful way is not to abandon the attempt, but rather to work toward greater precision and validity.

However, even those theorists who have attempted to bring organismically based needs into a unified theory of personality and culture have used a needlessly limited conception of human motivation. Primarily, they have been impressed with the simple physiological requirements of the organism. Thus, Kluckhohn and Murray (1956), in their introductory overview of the field, use the drives for food, oxygen, and sex as examples of constitutional determinants. Parsons and Shils (1962) similarly maintain that these "viscerogenic needs" serve as the basic substratum for socially determined acquired needs. Malinowski (1960), within the same general framework, also includes such biological needs as sleep, avoidance of pain, bladder pressure, health, temperature, and motility. As Malinowski said, "human beings have to live not by bread alone, but primarily by bread" (1944, p. 72). It is understandable that with such a reduced view of motivation little explanatory power has been found in organismically-based determinants. Little of the richness of cultural institutions can be helpfully explained by the need for food and oxygen. For this reason, the search for determinants has been forced to operate on the social level.

A much broader approach to this general problem has been taken recently by Spiro (1961), who argues that anthropologists should seriously consider the impact of psychological needs on cultural institutions. However, his concern is more with their function in the maintenance of a social system rather than with its origins. The only aspects of culture seen as structured by psychological needs are projective systems (i.e., religion), individual psychopathology, and culturally permissible roles of deviance. Actually, Spiro is more concerned with psychological defensive maneuvers in reaction to frustration by cultural norms than with the change in the norms themselves.

If it is true, as Spiro maintains, that frustrated psychological needs can exert this degree of influence, we soon come to agree that there are basic needs which are prior to culturally conditioned learning. If the only motives were those which culture produces for its own maintenance, frustration would not arise except in those cases of inappropriately learned motivation. This leads, then, to the question of why these presently accepted basic needs can lead only to additional, and culturally irrelevant, deviant roles. If basic needs can exert such power, then we must ask why they cannot exert some influence on structuring the primary cultural institutions themselves. At least, in principle, this further option exists and should be taken seriously. The addition of this possibility completes the broad concept of reciprocal psychological and cultural influence Spiro has proposed. It is, therefore, important to pose as a problem of research the power of psychological needs to affect all aspects of the culture.

MASLOW'S THEORY OF PERSONALITY

Although some anthropologists have acknowledged that isolated psychological needs may be relevant for cultural analyses, they have been less concerned with the relationship among the various needs. The human being has many needs, but not all are of equal moment. Needs are not amoeba-like, first flowing in one direction and then another, called forth by a particular requirement or opportunity, with no relationship to each other. Neither the neutral behavioristic model, nor the implicit use of single needs, such as sex, dominance or aggression, recognizes the patterning of motives to be found within the individual.

To integrate basic needs with socio-cultural determinants, it is necessary to turn to a personality theory whose concepts are rich enough to include much of the human drive system, and one which is, furthermore, explicit about the relationship between the various needs. One such approach is the theory of the "hierarchy of needs," outlined by Maslow (1954), which, I believe, holds out great possibilities for anthropological investigation.

Maslow proposes that the individual possesses a range of organismically-based needs. These fundamental motives are arranged in an ascending hierarchy of five need levels: (1) physiological; (2) safety; (3) love and belongingness; (4) self-esteem; (5) self-actualization. At each level the more basic needs must be relatively well-satisfied before the higher needs can become relevant to the individual. A brief summary of each level is presented below.[3]

The *Physiological* needs form the most basic level of motivation and are prepotent over the other needs. On this level are the needs of hunger, sex and thirst (the homeostatic mechanisms maintaining optimal levels of salt, sugar, temperature, oxygen, etc.) as well as the needs for sleep, relaxation, and bodily integrity. All of these must be satisfied before the organism can begin to function on higher levels. At this level are found those organismic needs which Malinowski, Parsons and Shils, and Kluckhohn and Murray have included in their theories of Culture and Personality.

When the physiological needs have been relatively well-satisfied, the individual becomes concerned with a new set, which are termed the *Safety* needs. These are

[3] A more detailed presentation of the theory may be found in Maslow's book, *Motivation and Personality* (1954).

centered around the requirement for a predictable and orderly world. The world must not appear unjust, inconsistent, unsafe, or unreliable. Maslow states that (for the child), "quarreling, physical assault, separation, divorce, or death within the family may be particularly terrifying" (1954, p. 86). If the safety needs have been deprived, the individual will feel insecure and mistrustful and will seek those areas of life which offer the most stability and protection. Further, he will attempt to organize his world to provide the greatest degree of safety and predictability possible.

After the physiological and the safety needs have been satisfied, there emerges the need to possess affectionate relationships with other people and to belong to a wider group. An individual, motivated on this level, desires warm and friendly human relationships and is able to function well in interpersonal situations. These are called the *Love* and the *Belongingness* needs.

The fourth level in the hierarchy constitutes the *Esteem* needs, defined as "first, the desire for strength, for achievement, for adequacy, for mastery and competence, for confidence in the face of the world, and for independence and freedom. Second, . . . the desire for reputation or prestige (defining it as respect or esteem from other people), status, dominance, recognition, attention, importance, or appreciation" (p. 90).

With the satisfaction of the lower needs the level of *Self-Actualization* is reached. This is described as the full use and exploitation of talents, capacities and potentialities. "Such people seem to be fulfilling themselves . . . [and] have developed or are developing to the full stature of which they are capable" (p. 201).

Maslow's theory of personality offers several important advantages for social explanation. First, the utilization of a theory of basic needs directs the field worker to a source of energy outside the cultural system, which may account for a great deal of human action and social organization. Thus, it is possible to find one of the major determinants of social phenomena rooted in the individual organism.

Second, in this formulation a wide range of human motivation has been organized into one general theory. The specific needs postulated by Maslow permit a much broader application of psychological theory to cultural phenomena than is possible with the more limited conceptualizations used by Malinowski, Kluckhohn and Murray, and Parsons and Shils. They permit the investigator to deal with behaviors ranging from simple physiological demands to complex social interaction. Furthermore, a commitment to a general psychological theory makes possible systematic comparison without the continual necessity to postulate new needs to fit each individual case.

Third, the concept of "prepotency" provides an important principle for understanding why specific cultural patterns emerge within a society. We can comprehend why people in a given milieu direct most of their activities toward the needs that have been frustrated, rather than in those that have already been satisfied, and why activities based on needs not yet relevant are conspicuously absent. In this way we are able to appreciate why many psychological and cultural patterns appear and how they are functionally related to each other. In the study to be reported below, my aim is to demonstrate both the difficulties involved in an analysis of a cultural system based solely on the sociocultural level, and the benefits to be derived from including within the set of determinants an exploration of the range of human needs and the process by which they press for gratification.

THE EXTREME POSITIONS
AND THE CONTEMPORARY SYNTHESIS

The extent and limits to which psychological and social systems influence or organize each other has been a recurring problem. Before presenting my own suggestions, and in order to pose the issue most sharply, I should like to review briefly certain of the more important positions which have been reached in working toward an integration. In so doing, my aim is not to provide a historical review of the field of Culture and Personality, but rather to discuss some of the major formulations and accentuate the theoretical issues.

Both fields have seen their radical reductionists. In

anthropology, Leslie White has made the most outspoken and sweeping attempt to order social reality in terms of the concept of culture, while in Freud and Geza Roheim we find the equivalent approach from the point of view of psychology. Both positions clarify, in their contrasts, the problems encountered and avoided in building an integrative theory from a unicausalist approach. Finally, it will be useful to examine the synthesizing work of John Whiting, which is the richest contemporary conceptualization of this problem.

Culturological Reductionism

Leslie White restates for contemporary anthropology a line of intellectual development which may be traced to the beginnings of systematic sociology. White sees the development of the sciences as a historical movement that brings human life under an ever-increasing order of inclusiveness. At each level, he argues, a new range of phenomena are brought into an organization which operates according to its own laws. White stresses that knowledge of what he calls lower-order sciences (such as physics, chemistry or psychology) is unnecessary for explanation on the sociocultural level. Culture, he argues, can only be explained in cultural terms.

> Customs and institutions—cultural traits in general—constitute a distinct class of phenomena. As such, it may be treated as a closed system. Culture is a thing sui generis; culture as culture can be explained only in terms of culture (*The Science of Culture*, 1949, p. 78).

White argues that culture is an organization dependent upon the symbolizing capacities of human beings and developed to serve their biological needs. Primarily, he claims, social organization exists to satisfy the biological requirements of subsistence, reproduction and protection. Once established, however, culture develops according to its own laws, and the individual person is therefore irrelevant to the cultural process. Although White argues that cultural analyses in psychological terms are a form of fallacious reductionism, he is emphatic in his insistence that cultural processes organize individual personality and behavior. In this way he maintains his own brand of reductionism based on the organizing properties of the "higher" level of cultural reality.

> Sometimes [the psychologist] declares that the institution exists because the people think and feel and act in a certain way; that the institution is merely the crystallization of certain psychological processes. He fails to realize that it is the other way around: the people feel, think and act the way they do because they possess—or, more accurately, are possessed by—a certain custom (1949, p. 77).

Although White does not deny the existence of psychological needs, he argues that they are irrelevent for cultural analyses because they cannot explain the variability of culture. This position is primarily based on a superficial conceptualization of the individual, for White's discussion of possible psychological determinants is usually in terms of such limited external physical features as height, color, or hair texture.

> The human species is of course varied, not uniform. There are tall peoples and short peoples; round heads and long heads; black, yellow, and white skins; straight, wavy and kinky hair; thick lips, long noses, and so on. . . . From a biological standpoint, the differences among men appear to be insignificant indeed when compared with their similarities. . . . As a matter of fact, it cannot be shown that any variation of human behavior is due to variation of biological nature. . . . Therefore, we may regard man as a constant, culture as a variable. . . . Thus we can explain the behavior of peoples in terms of their cultures; but we do not and cannot explain their cultures in terms of the respective "psychologies" of the peoples. The specific "psychologies" are psychosomatic expressions of the cultures, not their causes. The cultures must be explained in terms of culture; culturologically rather than psychologically (1949, pp. 123-5).

As an evolutionist, White deals with the difference between cultures. To a great extent, cultural differences can be attributed to differences in the technological order—which is his prime source of basic determinants. But a theory based on explaining differences between cultures does not necessarily include all the factors that may be involved in the development of any single one. Although White challenges psychology to explain the variability of culture, basically he is arguing that not only the variation but the particular culture itself cannot be explained in other than cultural terms. Furthermore, the human being is by no means the constant White presumes. There is still a degree to which variation can be attributed to varying processes in the organism.

By describing psychological determinants solely in terms of superficial biological characteristics, White avoids dealing with the biological energy systems. It is just in this area of motivation or drives that a further source of energy exists that might possibly be able to exert influence on the sociocultural system. It is, moreover, in the variability of the organismic drive system that one source of cultural variability may be found.[4]

Psychological Reductionism

Perhaps the most powerful statement of radical psychological reductionism is to be found in the writings of Freud and his anthropological disciple, Geza Roheim. Starting from their deep interest in intrapsychic phenomena, conceptualized as the experiences and vicissitudes of a particular drive system, they tended to view social organization primarily as psychology writ large.

In *Totem and Taboo*, Freud, assuming that the psychological processes of contemporary primitives and neurotics could be equated with those of primeval man—and thereby serve as a technique for historical reconstruction—formulated a social contract theory of the origin of culture based on the Oedipus complex. Beginning with Darwin's conclusion that the original human state was that of a horde ruled over by a powerful male, he took the ambivalent emotions toward the father which he had found in his patients and assigned them the chief role in the process through which culture was formed.

> There is only a violent, jealous father who keeps all the females for himself and drives away the growing sons. . . .

[4] It is important to realize that the concept of a hierarchy of needs answers Leslie White's objection that personality is a "constant" and therefore cannot explain in any way the variable "culture." White's position undoubtedly rests on the widespread anthropological assumption that culture (any culture) satisfies all of the human needs.

One day the expelled brothers joined forces, slew and ate the father, and thus put an end to the father horde. . . . The totem feast, which is perhaps mankind's first celebration, would be the repetition and commemoration of this memorable, criminal act with which so many things began, social organization, moral restrictions and religion.

[The] group of brothers banded together were dominated by the same contradictory feelings towards the father which we can demonstrate as the content of ambivalence of the father complex in all our children and in neurotics. They hated the father who stood so powerfully in the way of their sexual demands and their desire for power, but they also loved and admired him. After they had satisfied their hate by his removal and had carried out their wish for identification with him, the suppressed tender impulses had to assert themselves. . . . They undid their deed by declaring that the killing of the father substitute, the totem, was not allowed, and renounced the fruits of their deed by denying themselves the liberated women. Thus they created two fundamental taboos of totemism out of the sense of guilt of the son, and for this very reason these had to correspond with the two repressed wishes of the Oedipus complex (1938, pp. 915-17).

From the compromise reached by the "brothers," to erect a social organization to check aggressive and sexual impulses, Freud arrives at his fundamental definition of culture as an agency of instinctual repression. Once culture comes into existence there is little recognition in Freud's writings of the variety of social forms, or a theory of cultural transformations. To the extent that this issue is touched on at all, culture is discussed as a process of ever-increasing instinctual restriction. Although Freud discussed a few other social problems, he remained primarily concerned with the individual and never developed a genuine social psychology. It is only in the works of the anthropologist Geza Roheim that we find the results of a full-blown application of the Freudian system to cultural materials. Roheim's formulations are a somewhat expanded version of Freud's view that sociocultural organization is a direct expression of individual instinctual strivings.

From his assumption that culture is a mechanism by which the individual finds substitute gratifications for his infantile needs, Roheim concludes that the way to understand culture is through the study of psychological processes. "We see in every case a cultural element of some kind is explained on the basis of the same mechanisms that underlie the various kinds of neuroses" (1943, p. 25). He then expands the scope of cultural elements studied by Freud to include a discussion of economic institutions. Although recognizing the earlier arguments that economic factors could influence family structure and thus determine personality development (Abram Kardiner's, *The Individual and His Society*), Roheim maintained, nevertheless, that a direct analysis of economic institutions is possible by the application of psychoanalytic insights. "[The] course I am following in this paper is . . . to show the significance of phantasy or emotional life in shaping the economic situation, in other words, the activity of Id forces operating as Ego forces" (p. 40).

From this position he analyzes a number of economic institutions in terms of psychological forces. Thus, he argues that economic cooperation in marriage is not due to economic needs but to the maintenance of a stable sexual arrangement. The profession of the primitive medicine man "evolved on the bases of infantile body destruction phantasies" (p. 50). "The exchange of goods [trade] is . . . an externalized version of the exchange of body contents" (p. 53). The origins of agriculture lie in body destruction phantasies expressed in taking roots out of the ground, while the restitution phase of the phantasy led to planting and cultivation. He claims that gardening could not have originated because of its usefulness for "the result of inserting a tuber into the ground could not have been foreseen before it was tried" (p. 59). The agricultural use of the plough and ox evolved as genital impulses within the Oedipus and castration complex. Finally, domestication of animals such as the dog lies in the sublimated desire for love and companionship, and the acquisition of the cattle herd is determined by the Oedipus complex as a form of cattle totemism. He then concludes: ". . . having thus analyzed the main 'professions' of mankind, we find that they are all more or less distorted or projected equivalents of the infantile situation" (p. 72).

These simplistic examples give a good indication of the dangers involved in undertaking an analysis of culture from a unicausalist psychological foundation. Roheim's orientation remains, as does Freud's, in the study of individual psychological processes. His economic discussions are primarily based on myths and psychological anecdotes without seriously engaging in a structural analysis of economic organization. There is little attempt to search out historical, environmental or institutional factors that might account for the sociocultural elements under study. Moreover, as Roheim himself says, the psychological basis for the analysis is based on a limited instinctual underpinning of infantile needs and does not deal with the drives of the maturing individual. Yet, with all its oversimplification, this approach was extremely fruitful, for it raised the question of how unsatisfied instinctual forces find cultural means for gratification. It is, therefore, necessary to continue and extend the direction he has taken, examining in greater detail and with a broader scope the mutual relationship between the individual and his culture.

The Contemporary Integration

The most widely accepted conceptualization for ordering the phenomena in the area of culture and personality has been offered by John Whiting (1961). Whiting is unusual for an anthropologist in the seriousness of his attempt to grapple with psychological issues. Throughout much of his work, he has been concerned with the necessity of bringing psychological processes into the causal formulations of cultural institutions. His model, presented below, summarizes the relationships which he feels exist between the data of personality and culture.

Maintenance Systems	→	Child Training Practices	→	Personality Variables	→	Projective Systems

In this formulation the maintenance systems, by which Whiting refers to the economic modes of production, are primary in the process which establishes all aspects of the culture. The maintenance systems produce the broad framework of the culture's child training practices, and these, in turn, determine the personality of the child. The need state of the individual, produced by the child training practices, leads to the kind of projective systems —the specific forms of folklore, magic and religion— which exist in that culture.

In sum, this linear model places greatest emphasis on the economic arrangements of the culture, while little weight is given to psychological needs as antecedent variables in the process of culture-formation. The only institutions directly determined by individual need structure are the religious ones, and these are derivatives of the primary economic determinants. Such a conceptualization insists that personality is primarily the result of mechanisms designed to produce attitudes appropriate for the maintenance and transmission of the cultural pattern.

Whiting's formulation is vastly more sophisticated than that of Leslie White, as he provides a rich, detailed and concrete program of research into psychological processes as intermediary links in the cultural chain. In this way his work is a major step toward an integrated Culture and Personality. Nevertheless, this viewpoint is really not that far removed from the culturological formulations of White, as the two theories are fundamentally similar in denying the possibility that psychological needs can directly influence any aspect of the maintenance systems.

A MODEL FOR INTEGRATING PSYCHOLOGICAL AND SOCIOCULTURAL SYSTEMS

Because of the stress in contemporary theory on social factors in the organization of the social field, I should like to propose the following model as perhaps more clearly revealing the mechanism by which the integration between the psychological and social systems may take place. It is postulated that the cultural phenomena which the ethnographer observes result neither from cultural nor psychological determinants alone. Rather, they are the final products of an integration of the two in a particular setting. For a proper understanding of the structure and dynamics of either we cannot rely on a unicausalist mode of investigation, but rather must examine all the determinants and follow the process which has brought about this particular resolution. The research reported in this book will attempt to demonstrate the validity of this approach.

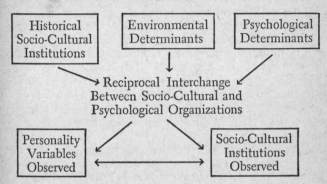

This hypothesis proposes that environmental features create the possibilities and set the limitations of cultural development. The sociocultural institutions brought to the area, including the political and social institutions, child training practices, value systems, technological apparatus and concepts of economic organization, adapt to the necessities of the land to produce preliminary institutional forms. These early forms are the first approximations of order based on the cultural material introduced to the area, and take into consideration the preliminary understanding of the environmental factors and the psychological characteristics of the population. As increased knowledge of the environment and the reactions of the human material in that particular setting is achieved, the cultural pattern first established re-adapts to take them into consideration.

During the time when the early cultural forms are being organized, the basic needs of the individual are gratified on some levels and deprived on others. If the degree of gratification possible under the early conditions leaves deficiencies in needs not yet provided for, the individual's deprived needs must find some form of satisfaction. They do so by restructuring the initial institutional forms into new patterns of organization in such a fashion as to get as much gratification for the need as possible.

This process of reciprocal interchange between the various determinants extends over a period of time, continually changing the relationship among its parts until a resolution has been reached. The ethnographer, studying a particular culture, observes the forms of both personality and culture that have been obtained by the action of all the determinants within that setting.

The process of reciprocal interchange usually cannot be observed, as the culture has likely developed its form long before his arrival. The setting that is most likely to give evidence of these events, and in which he can most readily come to grips with this process, of course, is one of a culture undergoing a period of significant change.

It should not be inferred that this process is viewed as if it occurred in complete isolation. Most cultures exist within a larger setting, and external influences continually impinge on all aspects of life. These influences can be interpreted within the set of proposed categories; for example, as changing the mechanism of the institutional determinants. In this way, they do not change the basic model of interaction that has been outlined.

It is my hope that the proposed model will not be seen as my own creation myth or "just so" story. The beginnings of cultural life are obviously impossible to study. What I am attempting is a delineation of the determining forces, or sources of energy, which direct the structuring of cultural and psychological organizations. This, in contrast, is pre-eminently open to investigation.

2

The Research Problem

To clarify the effect of psychological needs on cultural organization, I carried out a naturalistic field experiment which attempted to show the extent and limits of their power to structure cultural institutions. The verification of this hypothesis is based on two arguments. First, it is stated that the deprivation of a basic need will cause the individual to organize or utilize an institution in such a way as to achieve some measure of gratification for that deprived need. The study of that institution will show that it has been shaped to provide opportunities for such gratification. Second, it appears that human needs are arranged in an hierarchical order, which provides a basis for understanding why and when a given activity will appear. Upon study of an individual, it will be found that those who are concerned with gratification on a particular level will have been gratified on lower levels and will not be seeking gratification on higher levels. The institutions in which they are involved will follow this pattern.

There are three broad mechanisms by which the psychological need structure of the individual influences the specific form of the culture. First, the individual attempts to structure institutional means to provide direct gratification of his most relevant needs. Primarily, this will be the need level on which he has been most deprived, and which he is most concerned to gratify. Second, the level of psychological functioning sets and limits the range of cultural alternatives possible in a given ecological area. When the population cannot function beyond certain capacities, a barrier is raised to potential social developments. Third, when direct gratification of a psychological need results in a demographic fact or some unit of social structure, and these items (which are properly on the

18

sociological level) lead to the creation of further sociological phenomena, then causal explanation for these last phenomena (which are dependent on the intermediate social events) must be referred to the original psychological events that began the sequence.

If psychological needs are an independent factor in creating culture, then it is necessary to go beyond the usual examination of religious ideas or "projective systems" to a more general study of the economic and social institutions. Therefore, it is my purpose to analyze a particular culture and demonstrate the way in which the various determinants (environmental, psychological and sociocultural) affect one another and are integrated to produce the observed phenomena.

My plan of research was to find a small group of people among whom I could live and so be able to observe and participate in all aspects of their lives. This desire was ideally met in a rural village on the island of St. Kitts, in the British West Indies. I was fortunate to find a village that was the locus for two quite dissimilar occupations. This is unusual for St. Kitts, which has a monocrop economy devoted entirely to the cultivation of sugar cane. Together with the activities of the people involved in the dominant sugar cane estate, in this village there flourished a small but active group of fishermen. The presence of two occupational groups enabled me to set up a comparative study and examine each of the two economic organizations as a different subculture. The variations in structure of the economic organizations could then be studied and traced back to their several determinants. However, while fishing as an economic institution was totally in the hands of individual fishermen, the sugar cane estate was a large, complex and stratified organization. In order to establish a basis of comparison with the fishermen, it was necessary to isolate a comparable unit, at least in size, on the estate. For this reason the group of men who cut the sugar cane were selected. These two occupational groups, then, are the subject of this study.

Having tentatively established two subcultures, the organization of the cane cutting gang and the fishing crew was studied in detail. In this way the basic "maintenance systems," as Whiting terms them, were defined for study, and it became possible to determine the extent to which the psychological needs of the members of each group were influential as antecedent factors. In conjunction with this examination of an economic institution, I included a similar analysis of the structural features of the family for each of the two occupational groups. Family organization was chosen so that the theoretical issue might be posed as completely as possible, by bringing both economic and social organization into the study.

Each member of the two occupational groups residing in the village was studied in order to estimate his level of psychological functioning, in terms of Maslow's theory of personality. This allowed the motivational states of the groups to be compared and related to their economic and family structures. Further, some of their major childhood experiences, to which these psychological states might be attributed, were also examined.

In order to get a perspective on the historical and economic forces, which are usually cited as the sole cause of culture, a survey was made in the ethnographic material available of the forms the cane cutting gang and the fishing crew have taken in other West Indian areas. Through this review it was possible to pose the question of whether there is a compelling factor in the institutional structure of either occupation that, of necessity, would produce the specific organizational form found in the village studied.

METHODOLOGICAL PROCEDURES

My first contact with St. Kitts came in the summer of 1961, when my wife and I participated in a summer field work training program, sponsored by the Department of Anthropology at Brandeis University. Under this program, we initially spent a week and a half in the capital city of Basseterre meeting with many island leaders and explored a number of rural villages to find sites for our individual research. After this preliminary period of familiarization, we each chose a community we felt held potential for our projects. My wife and I decided on

Dieppe Bay, a lovely village on the northern shore. This was an extremely fortunate choice, although we were probably most influenced by its charm and the pleasant nature of our reception.

After entering the village, our greatest concern was to gain an understanding of the basic village institutions and win the confidence of the residents. To this goal we devoted the greatest part of our summer work. By the end of this period we had, at least, a general grasp of the estate structure and its influence on the lives of the village population, knowledge of some of the internal village social structure and a preliminary insight into the psychodynamics of some of the people with whom we had become friendly. We were also fortunate to benefit from the experiences of the other members of our group, which gave us an appreciation for the island-wide influences on all the rural villages.

After two and a half months the program came to an end and our group returned to the United States. During the ensuing year our research was discussed in a seminar devoted to St. Kitts given by the Department of Anthropology at Brandeis. It was during these discussions that the theoretical problem took on importance and crystallized into its present form. We also corresponded with many of the village residents, in order to maintain contact and continue their familiarization with us.

We returned to the village in September, 1962. By this time we had a general knowledge of the island and village and were known to most of the village residents; we could turn, therefore, to a focused examination of the specific sociocultural units we had selected for study. Our aim was to make an intensive analysis of the cane cutting gang and the fishing crew, and the family structures developed by these individuals. The hope was that such an examination of a limited group would yield data rich enough to put the theoretical hypothesis to a test. Given our limitations of time this was felt preferable to a more inclusive but superficial survey of the entire population.

My criteria for the selection of subjects were simple. It was decided that all the cane cutters and fishermen resident in Dieppe Bay were to be studied. As there were twenty-one cutters and nineteen fishermen in the village it was possible to work with the entire population and not become involved with sampling difficulties. However, the cane cutters studied were a sample in one way, in that the cane gangs in which they worked were also staffed by men from similar neighboring villages. While it is true that the procedure chosen prevented these other men from being studied, there was no reason to expect them to be different from the cane cutters of Dieppe Bay. To this extent the cane cutters studied are a sample of the cane cutters of this area. This criterion of selection was felt to be superior to the alternative of sampling all the cutters on the estate, because as we lived in their village, we had become friends with many of them.

After spending three months in Dieppe Bay, I developed a series of questions on which it was necessary to get detailed and equivalent information from all subjects. This was termed the Male Interview, and may be found in Appendix I, with the other objective instruments used. My procedure was to seek out, individually, all the cane cutters and fishermen residing in Dieppe Bay, and, either in the privacy of their homes or mine, read the questions to them and note their answers on the interview form. For the most part, I knew all of these men, and many quite intimately. In this way the standardized interview was very different from the usual questionnaire technique. For one thing, I had spent five months over a period of a year and a half becoming acquainted with them. The interview was introduced and, I believe, regarded by these people as merely the extension of our many hours of unstructured conversation. Further, I also felt free to permit answers to develop into conversations and to digress whenever interesting leads appeared. In this way many of the anxieties produced by questionnaires as well as their inherent impersonality were avoided.

The responses to the Male Interview were analyzed in November and December of 1962. In the middle of December I became ill and was forced to return to the United States. I returned to complete the study in March, 1963. This interval was also an opportunity for reviewing the material I had gathered and posing new directions for study.

When I returned, I continued the ethnographic investigation of work-group organizations and family structure and developed two further data-collecting instruments. To determine the personality structure of the cane cutters and fishermen empirically, I devised a projective test based on the issues that seemed relevant to me from my contacts with these men.[1] This test included both sentence completions and projective questions and was given to all the men whom I had previously questioned on the Male Interview. In the period that had elapsed between the interview and the projective test several changes in the population had occurred. New men entered these activities, others left the village and some had taken sick. None of these men were given the projective test because I was trying to keep as many of the fluctuating variables as constant as possible. For this reason the size of the projective sample is somewhat smaller than the interview sample. On the projective test both groups were reduced by four men each, for a total of seventeen cane cutters and fifteen fishermen. The omissions, however, do not seem to have changed the composition of the groups in any significant way.

The one external factor which might have had a significant influence was the difference in the seasonal patterns of employment. In the end of March and beginning of April, when the test was given, the cane cutters had had three months of peak income while the fishermen were just emerging from their "dead" season. The winter for the fishermen is a time of stormy seas when little fishing can be done, and many of their fish pots are lost. The effect of this differential in experience should serve to dampen the predicted difference between the two groups. If anything, it should raise the cane cutters on the hierarchy of needs while lowering the fishermen. That the two groups still showed major differences in the predicted direction is all the more striking.

The projective test was constructed in the field, and I

[1] I wish to acknowledge the benefit derived from my review of tests used by (Whiting, J. W. M., et al., in press). Doob (1960) and Rubin (n.d.). Certain of their materials were used in this test. See Appendix III.

experimented with possible stems and questions in a pilot study with village residents other than my subjects. Many items produced stereotyped answers or else were found to be phrased inappropriately. These were either reformulated or dropped entirely from the test. The pilot study was also valuable in that it brought out the problems I would face giving a projective test to Kittitians. For example, I discovered that this population did not know the meaning of the word "sentence," which presents great problems when instructions for a sentence completion test are given! As was the case with the Male Interview, I read the stem and wrote the responses on the test form. All tests were given individually either in their home or mine.

I also felt that it was necessary to get standardized information from the women of these men and so devised a Female Interview[2] which my wife, who is an anthropologist, carried out for me. The Female Interview was given in the same manner as the Male and included many equivalent questions. As it was given in the last stages of field work it also provided an opportunity to gather certain information about the men or about their families as a unit, which had only become relevant as the research progressed. In all, this interview was given to twenty-seven women.

The number of informants will be seen to change in the different tables in which the information gathered by these standardized techniques is presented. The reasons for this are varied. Occasionally, an informant would refuse to answer or would get too involved in one point to be able to handle others. Sometimes, at my discretion, I omitted a question because I felt it inappropriate for that person, or because the informant was tiring. Other variations are due to the changing number of people who are relevant for different topics, e.g., married men, Kittitians, men who know their fathers, etc. Finally, there are some cases where the answers recorded are simply not relevant to the method of analysis. There was no way to force a subject to be focused if he had something else he wanted to say or was searching for a way to avoid the

[2] See Appendix II.

question. Fortunately, these variations were infrequent, but as they did occur a changing N resulted.

In this study it will be noted that much of the usual report in Culture and Personality investigations is absent. There will be little discussion of such things as feeding, toilet training and early sex practices, which bulk so large in most discussions. The primary reason for these omissions is that the study has been constructed to examine carefully those persons who are involved in specific units of social organization. I have not attempted to create an hypothesized Kittitian, Dieppe Bay-ian or even cutter and fisherman. This is a methodological point of great importance. The customary practice is to produce individual personality studies, a generalized child-rearing survey gathered from contemporary sources (a mother-child interview) and an exposition of social structure; and then, depending on the theoretical position, to point out relationships among these variables.

For the purpose of this investigation this usual procedure would probably produce irrelevant results. Since cane cutters (whose occupation is but one of many on the estate) and fishermen are not hereditary castes but, rather, contemporary occupational categories, it would be impossible to determine which mothers to interview in hopes of discovering what the childhood of a cane cutter or fisherman was like. According to present studies, child-rearing practices discovered are assumed to be those experienced by the adults studied. While this approach is probably valid for relatively stable societies or for broad questions involving large homogeneous groups, it is completely inappropriate for this study. Therefore, it was decided, in view of the impossibility of longitudinal examination over whole lifetimes, to use the data that may be gleaned from retrospective questioning of the individual under study.

We left Dieppe Bay in the beginning of May, 1963. In all, we spent a total of nine months in the village over a period of two years. This enabled us to witness the entire annual cycle of events and follow the progress of social change the island is experiencing. Although the field work had to be carried out in three periods, this necessity gave us the benefit of a longer term involvement with the community, an opportunity to review and reformulate many of the research questions and extended our process of acquaintanceship with the residents of Dieppe Bay. Each return, it seemed, gave proof of our interest in them and immeasurably strengthened our ability to work in their midst.

3

The Setting

In this chapter I shall present an outline of the environmental, historical, technological and demographic conditions within which the contemporary social field has developed. My aim is to provide the basic information dealing with the first stage in the theoretical model—the environment and past-socioeconomic institutions which entered into the reciprocal interchange with the psychological determinants. This will necessarily be a selective discussion, as this work is neither an historical nor ethnographic study of St. Kitts as a whole.[1]

ECOLOGY

St. Kitts is a semi-tropical volcanic island centrally situated in the Leeward Islands. Roughly oval in shape, with a long arid peninsula extending to the southeast, it is a small fertile island with an area of 68 square miles. Down the center of the island ranges a chain of mountains, the highest of which, Mt. Misery, rises to 3,711 feet. The mountains slope gently into the sea and are intensively cultivated with sugar cane well onto the more steeply graded upper slopes. Above this line, where the incline is too precipitous to permit the movement of machinery, is a narrow region where the laborers are granted small garden plots by the estates to work on a share-crop basis. The remainder of the mountains are heavily wooded and carefully protected by the plantations in the interest of conservation.

Throughout the island a series of ravines, locally known as guts, extends from the summit of the mountains down

[1] Much of this information has been gathered from two recent studies of St. Kitts by G. Merrill (1958) and M. Aronoff, N. Raymond and B. Melemed (1962), which may be referred to for a more detailed account of the island.

27

to the sea. Except just after a rain, when heavy torrents of water course down through them, they are quite dry. As the ravines are the only land unsuitable for cultivation, they have long been the sites of the workers' villages. Because there are few permanent springs and only one permanent stream, St. Kitts has had to rely on the collection of rain in reservoirs for its water supply. However, in contrast to several other West Indian islands, this suppply, from a rainfall averaging 54 inches annually, has always provided the island with sufficient water to insure the high productivity of the land.

A detailed discussion of the soils of St. Kitts may be found in Merrill's book. They are succinctly described by a commission examining the sugar industry (Soulbury, 1949, p. 2) as follows: "The soils of St. Kitts, derived from deposits of volcanic ash, are deep, easily worked, light, sandy loams, with free natural drainage. They are somewhat lacking in mineral salts, but their good drainage and the ease with which they can be worked render them admirably suited to the growing of sugar cane." For our purposes it is sufficient to recognize that with the addition of organic fertilizers the soils are good enough to encourage the cultivation of sugar cane. The quality of the soil, combined with the adequacy of rainfall, gives St. Kitts opportunities for intensive sugar cane cultivation unusual for such a small island. Due to these factors St. Kitts has continued to rely on the sugar plantation system when most of the other small West Indian islands were forced out of business by competition with the large-scale sugar cultivation on the big islands, such as Cuba and Jamaica.

The excellence of the soil and the small area available for cultivation led the planters to exploit almost all the land for the cultivation of sugar cane. By 1954, 97% of the arable land was devoted to its production. From the standpoint of the laborers this has led to several unfortunate results. In contradistinction to many other West Indian areas, such as British Guiana, Trinidad, Guadeloupe, and Barbados, it proved impossible for the slaves, after emancipation, to move off the plantations to unused crown lands where they could establish villages on individually owned land. In later chapters I shall discuss in detail the psychological benefits that derive from escaping estate control. Moreover, the retention of virtually all land by the estates for the cultivation of sugar cane made it impossible for the laborers to acquire plots of land for growing vegetables and pastures on which to graze livestock. Since the laborers can own no land they are totally dependent upon the estates for their entire income and are subject to marked underemployment for almost half of the year. Such dependence on the seasonal nature of employment, plus the high cost of food, has resulted in a poor diet, heavily overbalanced with starches, which has increased the population's vulnerability to disease. Further, the use of virtually all land by the estates has forced the workers to construct their houses in the dank ravines which are natural breeding grounds for various diseases. Only in the past few years has the government instituted a policy of purchasing prime cane fields from the estates to build new villages.

HISTORY

St. Kitts was discovered by Columbus in 1493 and colonized by a group of Englishmen under Thomas Warner in 1623. The native Caribs offered little resistance to the settlers, who soon began to establish themselves as small-scale farmers. During the next century and a half, until the English finally took lasting possession of St. Kitts under the Treaty of Versailles in 1783, control of the island followed the vicissitudes of the colonial wars, shifting back and forth between the English, Spanish and French. For one period, from 1629 to 1706, the island was partitioned, with the English holding the middle, and the French, both ends. Colonists of both countries, however, set their quarrels aside and united temporarily in 1627 to drive the Caribs from the island.

The earliest white settlers cleared the land and set out small-scale tobacco holdings. However, there soon developed a glut on the world market and prices fell sharply. In 1639 the colonists experimented with indigo, but this too proved unsuccessful. It was in the 1640's that sugar was introduced, which opened the way to prosperity for the Kittitian planter. Cultivation of sugar cane was not merely a change in crop, but an innovation which brought about a radical revision in the organization of agriculture. To grow sugar cane profitably the small holdings had to be consolidated into larger estates, labor had to be brought in and, as sugar cane demands immediate processing, the plantation owner had to become a manufacturer as well.

Large-scale production required major capital investments either by the planter or through loans from English sugar merchants, and ownership of the land shifted to those persons who had access to these funds. In order to pay off these loans and obtain a profit, the planters attempted to structure the organization of the estate in the most economically rational manner.

At first the landowners sought to attract white indentured servants, who came with the hope of eventually winning their own lands. But the rapid development of large estates soon engulfed all the available land and so dried up the indentured labor source. The planters then requested the Lords of Trade and Plantations to send out prisoners, but few reached St. Kitts. Although there was a brief influx of political prisoners after the Monmouth Rebellion, the planters soon came to realize that these sources were both unpredictable and insufficient. They then turned to the Dutch dealers in the Negro slave trade, and when the demand for slaves became intense the British founded their own Royal African Company in 1670. This gave the estate owners a dependable pool of laborers who could be permanently attached to an estate.

Upon this basis the Kittitian plantation system was founded, and much of its early form continues to dominate the economy to the present day. The introduction of Negro slaves also has determined the contemporary racial composition of the island. According to the 1946 census, 98% of the population is listed as Black or Colored.

In 1807 the slave trade was abolished, and in 1833 the slaves on St. Kitt were emancipated. Throughout the West Indies the slaves responded by an immediate movement away from the estates and estate control. On many islands there was a severe shortage of labor, which impelled the planters to experiment with the importation of indentured Chinese and East Indian laborers. On the smaller islands, like St. Kitts, little unused land was available to which the emancipated slaves could move, and out of necessity they were forced to continue to work for their former owners. For them the effect of emancipation was, at first, more a change of legal status than a chance at economic advancement. The sole visible change was a shift of residential pattern away from estate yard to the unarable land in the guts, and the rocky and often precipitous slopes along the shore.

Nevertheless, through emancipation, the former slaves acquired freedom of choice and movement. This gave them the power to bargain with the planters over the conditions of their labor, a process that culminated in the formation of a labor union a century later. Emancipation also permitted them to leave St. Kitts when they learned of more attractive conditions elsewhere, and the history of the latter part of the 19th and the 20th century is a tale of continuous emigrations to the Canal Zone, Cuba, Trinidad, the Dominican Republic, the United States, Britain, and, at present, the American Virgin Islands (Proudfoot, 1950).

While emigration greatly improved the conditions of those individuals who were able to leave, it has been one of the most significant factors intensifying the instability and precariousness of life on St. Kitts. Although those who left frequently sent money to their families and friends, from the point of view of those left at home their departure was often disastrous. Emigration dislocated family life further by separating fathers and mothers from their children, and resulted in the placement of a large number of children with "foster" parents. In later chapters I shall discuss in detail the events which often took place and the resulting psychological damage to the child. Moreover, as those who emigrated were usually men (*Ibid.* p. 92), from at least 1871 on there has been a constant female surplus which has further weakened the ability of the female to establish a stable family. Although until recently adequate emigration statistics have not been recorded, from our knowledge that the surplus of females is due to male emi-

TABLE 3-1

Population of St. Kitts, 1871-1960

	1871	1881	1891	1901	1911	1921	1946	1960
Males	13,259	13,706	14,410	12,977	10,969	9,014	13,582	18,074
Females	14,910	15,431	16,466	16,805	15,314	13,401	16,252	20,217
TOTAL	28,169	29,137	30,876	27,782	26,283	22,415	29,834	38,291
Male/Female Ratio	89:100	89:100	88:100	77:100	72:100	67:100	84:100	89:100

gration, we can get a rough estimate of the degree of movement by examining the population statistics presented in Table 3-1.

From the viewpoint of emigration as a significant influence in the lives of the men I studied, whose average age is 40 years, it is interesting to note that the period of greatest male/female imbalance came in the year 1921.[2] Although the next official census was taken in 1946, Kuczynski (1953), whose demographic work is the standard reference for the British Commonwealth, estimates that in 1938 the population of St. Kitts had diminished to 17,886. Unfortunately, he does not give the male/female ratio, but as we know that a sharply reduced population figure is due primarily to male emigration, we may conclude that the process of emigration, which had begun at the end of the 19th century, continued up to the beginning of the Second World War, when movement was frozen. It is during this period, from 1910-1940, that most of the men in my sample were born and reared.[3]

DIEPPE BAY

1. *History*

The village of Dieppe Bay, on the northern shore, was among the earliest settlements on St. Kitts. The year

[2] The validity of using the male/female ratio as an index of male migration is confirmed by examining this ratio at various age levels. Such an analysis is necessary to insure that the imbalance is not due to an unusual sex ratio differential at birth, or an extreme male susceptibility to disease in childhood. The ratio below the age of 15 is 96:100 in the year 1921. Between the ages of 15 to 49, however, for that year it drops to 52 males for every 100 females. This breakdown by age thus indicates that the ratio in the total population of 67:100 in 1921 covers up what is an even more striking sex imbalance among the adult population of St. Kitts.

[3] The effects of the emigration on the children may be seen in a census taken in the neighboring village of St. Pauls, in 1961. Covering the entire population of that village, it was determined that 66% of the children under 12 were not living in a household with their father, and 31.5% were not living with their mother. (Personal communication from Nathaniel Raymond.)

after Thomas Warner founded the colony, a damaged French privateer landed to make repairs at what is now Dieppe Bay. Warner, at that time, feared attack from the Caribs and invited the French to stay and help defend the European settlement. Three years later this arrangement was formalized by a treaty partitioning the island, with the English taking the middle portion and the French both ends. The French captain named the settlement for his home town of Dieppe, and after partition it served as the capital of the northern division.

Under both French and English control, Dieppe Bay has been an important governing town. A barrier reef lying offshore, forming the only safe shelter on the windward side, is the primary reason for its prominence. As soon as the estates were established, Dieppe Bay became the port to which ships came, bringing in food, machinery, household furnishings, and taking out the sugar manufactured by the estates. Even after the central factory was built in Basseterre, in 1912, the estates in this region continued to transport their unprocessed sugar canes to Dieppe Bay for re-shipment by small boat to the factory. It was not until the last sections of the railroad reached the neighboring estates, in 1923, that the value of the safe harbor to the northern region was diminished and Dieppe Bay lapsed into the life of a typical rural village, whose main function is to house estate laborers.

But its unique historical position left several important legacies. As a port, Dieppe Bay had a life apart from the estates. Many merchants settled there, bought land, raised large houses and conducted a variety of businesses. At one time there were warehouses, lumber yards, and artisans' shops serving the estates in the area and the ships which frequently called. Today, the result of this commercial period is that, in contrast to the other rural villages, some land is privately owned and large buildings exist that the government can use for district governmental functions. Having once been an administrative town for economic reasons, Dieppe Bay continued to attract multivillage agencies, such as a court, a police station, a post office, a clinic and a tiny library.

2. *The Village*

Today, Dieppe Bay is a quiet little village, of approximately one thousand inhabitants, extending for about a quarter of a mile along one side of the main road. From this road three streets descend toward the sea, and along these streets, closely set together, are the more prosperous homes and shops. Also, along these main streets are the government school, the churches and a large building housing the post office, police station and district court. Between these streets wind dirt alleyways and footpaths among a crowd of small one- and two-room wooden houses. To the southeast is a cocoanut grove and the estate pasture stretching for about a half mile to the next village. In the pasture has been set the estate yard with its stables, storehouses and manager's quarters. Nearby, is a group of three small concrete buildings housing the district nurse, sanitary officer, and clinic. Dominating the area, and surrounded by a high stone wall, is the large home of the estate owner. Along the Atlantic boundary, fronting on the protected lagoon, is a narrow strip of sand, used by the village fishermen to beach their boats.

Dieppe Bay is, then, a village tightly compressed between the road and the ocean, situated on privately owned land around the harbor. Across the road from the village begin the cane fields, composed of fields in various stages of growth, separated by a grid of dirt roads used by the tractor-hauled cane carts. The fields extend across the gently sloping apron of the island and follow the slopes of the mountain until the grade becomes too steep for the passage of tractors. At this elevation, about two miles from the village, the estate rents out small plots of land (¼ acre) for growing vegetables to some of its laborers. Historically, there has been a controversy over whether or not the estate will rent sufficient land to support a family which does not choose to work for the estate. In any event, distribution of these rented plots is the estate's prerogative and certainly one of its mechanisms of control.

Except for the small house plots along the streets, there

is no privately owned land in Dieppe Bay, as the estates, pressed for arable land, took control of whatever was available. This land shortage forced a residential pattern of dense housing, and a minimal amount of pasturage for grazing livestock. It also prevented the estate laborers from developing the system, which exists in many other West Indian sugar cane growing areas (see Chapter 6), of combining estate labor with cultivation of significant (2-5 acre) plots of their own land.

3. Population Classes

The large majority of the men and women of Dieppe Bay are laborers who find their livelihood in some capacity on the estate. All are bound to the vicissitudes of a cane economy, with a crop season of intensive labor and a dull season of major under-employment. The annual cycle of events on the estate determines the course of village activities and, except for those who have been able to emigrate, their goals and life styles have had to be worked out within the framework of what the estate can provide.

One village group that has been able to escape from the dictates of the estate system contains the men who have utilized the sea's resources and have made fishing their occupation. Although in terms of income, ethnicity, and status they are identical with the majority of the village population, they have been able to develop a life pattern diverging in many significant respects from the island norm. One aspect of this study will explore how they differ from the bulk of the population and why they have come to deviate from the usual cultural pattern.

In addition to the laborers there is a group that through education, family connections and personal qualities has been able to rise to a higher income and standard of living, and a higher position in the island's social structure. These "include craftsmen, such as carpenters, masons and seamstresses, and also bus drivers, clerks, shopkeepers, teachers, policemen, ministers and a union organizer. All live in Dieppe Bay, but many commute daily to Basseterre where they work in government or private employ" (M. Aronoff, 1962). Whatever leadership exists in the village derives from this group. The children's youth groups, the church groups, community councils (now defunct), the island-wide garden festival and even the local branch of the labor union all look to the ministers, teachers and artisans for organization and stimulation. In actuality, this class provides most of the membership as well as leadership and exercises jealous control over the criteria of participation.

The bulk of the village population, including its children, is more or less excluded from these formal groups, and looks to the rum shops and shopkeepers for its social activity. These shops often provide a separate room with a juke box where the men can dance, play dominos or congregate in informal evening gatherings. In Dieppe Bay there are four of these rum shops, as well as a number of other shops that stock only food. The shopkeepers in Dieppe Bay are often looked up to by the laborers and fulfill the important role of moderating quarrels, furnishing advice, and, occasionally, lending money.

Intruding into the village affairs, but never part of the daily interchange, are the activities of the highest status groups, such as the estate owners, lawyers, doctors, government officials and the personnel of the large-scale commercial establishments. Their efforts are vital to the existence of the village, for they create and direct the sugar industry's functions both on the island and in the world market. Although this study will be concerned with the limited problems of the local economic and social institutions of the rural workers, the larger context in which life in Dieppe Bay is maintained must not go unmentioned.

THE SUGAR ESTATE

Sugar cane cultivation on St. Kitts has been organized along the lines of the capitalistic plantation system. The trend, historically, has been to increase the size of the estates and operate them on the most economically rational basis within the owner's power. At present there are 47 estates on St. Kitts, of which 27 are owned and operated by corporations, while most of the remainder are run by resident planters. Compared with plantations found in other areas of the world, these estates tend to be small, ranging in size from 100 to 800 acres.

Coordinating the policies of all the estates are two

formal organizations: the St. Kitts Sugar Producers Association, which embraces all the estate owners and negotiates wage rates with the labor union; and the St. Kitts Sugar Association, composed of estate owners, processors and businessmen involved in the industry, which carries on research, suggests agricultural practices and standards, and negotiates quotas and prices in the external sugar market. The third island-wide institution is the St. Kitts-Nevis Trades and Labor Union, established in 1940, which negotiates wages for the entire work force and represents the estate laborers in their disputes with individual estate owners.

The hub of the sugar industry is the central factory in Basseterre, established in 1912 to take over the manufacturing processes which had previously been the individual estate owner's responsibility. Before it was built each estate operated its own small processing plant, run by either windmills or animal power. These were never as efficient as the central factory, whose skill and efficiency, it is said, saved the sugar industry of St. Kitts and today permits it to compete with the major sugar-producing regions of the world. The central factory, which built a narrow-gauge railway line around the island to transport the cane and to assure a regular flow of cane, regulates every estate's reaping activities by providing only enough railroad cars each day to carry a fixed quota of cane. In this way the harvesting schedules of all estates have been thoroughly coordinated. When emergencies arise on individual estates the factory diverts additional railroad cars to them, thereby bringing harvesting activity on the other estates to a stop. No estate would want to stockpile cane for eventual transport and have the juice evaporate under the hot sun.

The estate, itself, is a stratified and tightly organized institution. On approximately half of the estates there is a resident owner who may or may not concern himself with the details of managing. The key to the estate functioning is the manager, who must organize and supervise all aspects of the work. He may be the owner of the estate, although usually he is an employee. Like the owners on St. Kitts, he may be either colored or white. It is his responsibility to plan all the activities of cultivation—the planting, weeding, fertilizing, reaping and shipping of the cane. He is also involved in allocating estate lands for house sites and garden plots, keeping records of the estate expenditures and personally issuing the weekly wages to the laborers.

Generally, he passes instructions down to the overseer and limits himself to inspecting field operations from a jeep once or twice a day. The field overseer is in charge of actually supervising the work and spends most of the day on horseback circulating among the various work crews. His duties consist of settling major disputes, if they should arise, and examining the quality and maintaining the pace of the work. The overlooker, who walks, is the last of the administrative hierarchy, and his duties mostly involve supervising the loading of the cane onto the railroad cars, and checking on the weeding, hoeing and fertilizing done by the older men, women and boys.

The cultivation of sugar cane encompasses a variety of tasks. During crop time, from January to August, the estate's efforts are totally engaged in reaping the cane and sending it down to the factory. The most strenuous burden falls to those who cut the cane. On St. Kitts this is usually done by large work crews called "gangs," composed of nine to eleven of the best workers. Each gang is led by one of its members, the "head cutter," who sets the pace and has direct responsibility for the gang's production. His is the classic economic status of the foreman; he is not in the administration, yet is somewhat distant from his fellow workers. The estate I studied had three cutting gangs staffed by the vigorous adult men, and two composed of older men and boys learning the skill. As the men cut their way through the fields, they throw the stalks in piles which are then loaded in carts hauled by tractors. Formerly, loading the cane into these carts was done by a separate group of men, called "handers." In 1961, the large estates introduced a mechanical loader which took over this job and displaced these men. However, handers still work with the older men and boys. After the cane is dumped into the carts the tractors pull them down to a siding on the railroad line where they are put into railroad cars and sent to the factory. On my first visit, in 1961, the cane was transferred by a separate group of men, the "packers," whose job was to strip the cane stalks of any leaves overlooked by the cutters and skillfully pack the cane into the railroad cars. In 1962, they, too, suffered technological unemployment as the estates brought in a large crane to lift the cane out of the carts and dump it into the railroad cars.

After the crop has been reaped there is usually a few weeks' slack period during which very little work is available. Then slowly the estate begins to prepare the fields for the next season, and men are given jobs rebuilding the cane banks, clearing the fields, spreading fertilizer and planting cane. This is the dull season, life slows down on the estate and in the village, tractors stop racing down the main street, and men spend considerable time sitting and waiting for the next crop. Generally, even the most valued workers can expect no more than two and a half days' work each week and earn only about a third of their former income. During this period many men devote their time to plots of vegetable grounds they have rented in the mountain where they raise enough provisions to tide them over until the beginning of crop.

There are a variety of other jobs on the estate which must, at least, be mentioned in this overview. Some men have a year-round job looking after the estate animals, working in the estate yard, or driving tractors. The older men work by the day weeding and caring for the fields. The women also weed and spread fertilizer, working both singly and in gangs. All those activities, too, have undergone transformation as the process of mechanization on the estate has included the change to chemical fertilizers and weedicides.

FISHING

Centered around the harbor a number of men have developed a means of existence in large measure independent of the dominant sugar estates. As far back as 1871, when fishermen were listed in the census, and probably still earlier than that, Dieppe Bay was the atypical locus of a small fishing trade. Although it is difficult to establish the historical nature of fishing from the census records, one may assume that under slavery fishing was not

encouraged; the estates preferred to import food and re-
serve their slaves for more profitable labor in the cane
fields. Possibly, a few slaves were allocated to procure fresh
fish for the estate owner, but the independent development of a fishing trade had to wait upon emancipation.
Even then, from the census records, there has never been
a major utilization of the resources of the sea, as has been
the case in other West Indian islands.

Today, a group of nineteen men have chosen to devote themselves to the sea, and in so doing have developed a subculture which is remarkably different from
the Kittitian norm. For these men the beach is the center
of their lives. Most of their houses are located nearby,
and they spend their working and leisure time close to
the sea. In this way, too, they have geographically clustered and separated themselves as much as possible from
the sugar estate. This is not to say that the fishermen
never visit other parts of the village, or that estate laborers do not also live near the bay. But, for the fishermen,
most of their time is spent near the beach area, repairing
equipment, or socializing, dancing and playing dominos
in a large rum shop at the foot of the street near the sea.
They have even formally organized a domino club, composed only of fishermen, which nicely symbolizes their
separation from the dominant estate culture.

The fishermen's life, like the cane cutters', also follows
the natural rhythm of the seasons, with intense periods of
labor followed by periods of relatively little work. In the
beginning of March, after the seas have begun to calm,
the fishermen, working in crews of three and four, set
out their wire fishpots in about a mile and a half radius
from the village. For the most part they use 12-15 foot
wooden rowboats, although there are, at present, two sail-
boats, and set their pots to trap a variety of fish which
feed near the rocks, such as snapper, grunt, thumb, but-
terfish, doctorfish, old wife, hind and parrot fish. They also
set out nets to trap turtle and shark. The potfish season
reaches its height in April, June, and July and then
begins to taper off in the fall. By Christmas, the seas
begin to get rough and virtually no fishing is done outside
the harbor until March. In August, large schools of
garfish visit the waters off Dieppe Bay and the fishermen,

together with some cane workers who come down to the bay after the end of harvest, form crews of four and five men to fish the gar with long seines. By December, the garfish season, too, has ended and the fishermen have little to do until the seas go down in March. During this period of forced leisure the fishermen spend a few weeks building new fish pots to replace the ones lost or worn out during the season. Both to buy new pots and to carry themselves over this dull season, they draw upon money they saved up during the year. Since there is no other source of income during their dull season, saving money is an essential feature of their lives.

What is most astonishing about the fishing trade in Dieppe Bay is its small size. Soon after I arrived in the village I wondered why there were not more men who took up fishing for a living. Logically, there should have been a much larger and more active group of fishermen, for the market, the capital, the equipment, the resources, the economic and psychological return are all present.

It is important to examine this carefully as it has much to teach about the principles of fishing in Dieppe Bay. To demonstrate the nature of this paradox we must review each of the economic requirements which would lead to the expectation of a more extensive fishing industry.

First, the market. The villagers continually complain that there is not enough fresh fish available and that those who are fortunate enough to purchase what is brought in have to be either of higher status, relatives of fishermen, or those in a position to do them favors. As a result, their diet tends to be heavily overbalanced with starch, and contains very little protein. It is symbolic of the lack of protein that the word used for meat and fish in St. Kitts is "relish," in the sense that they usually buy a tiny piece of salt meat or fish to flavor their pot of boiled starches. Nor is it true that they favor starch and dislike meat. When we asked the women of the cane cutters what kind of "relish" they preferred, 14 of the 15 women vociferously maintained that they preferred fresh fish and condemned salt fish and meats with comments like "salt stuff burns the stomach." Most of these women also complained that is was very difficult to purchase any fish. To establish the extent of the potential market in Dieppe Bay, we made a survey of the shopkeepers to find out how much salt fish and meat and frozen chicken each shop sold each year. The amount of sales in the village came to a total of 15,000 lbs., sold at a rate two to three times higher per pound than fresh fish. Whereas fresh fish sells at 32¢ per pound,[4] salt fish costs 60¢ per pound and salt meat costs $1.00 per pound. If the neighboring villages, which have no direct access to fresh fish are included, the potential market for Dieppe Bay fish, estimated solely in terms of the present consumption of high price salt fish and meats, reaches 85,500 lbs. per year. As the average weekly income of a fisherman is approximately $20, the total harvest in Dieppe Bay may be estimated at about 40,000 lbs. of fish per year. This differential shows that production could double or triple just to fill the presently existing demand.

The second factor is the resources in the sea. No scientific survey has been made of the waters off Dieppe Bay, but from several other sources it is safe to conclude that the potential has not been reached. The Fisheries Department has made spot checks of these waters, and I was assured that a much greater industry could develop if the population was so inclined. This was also the opinion of the most experienced fishermen, who felt that the sea could support at least twice the present number of fishermen. Furthermore, most of the fishermen limit their range to about a mile and a half of the sea. Few travel down the east coast of the island. Those who do take some of the largest hauls among the fishermen and report many untapped and lucrative banks which could support many more fishermen. The last indication of resources comes from the fact that the men who take the largest catches are those who are most ambitious to raise their standard of living. We can assume therefore that if the rest of the fishermen, or other individuals in the village, had the same psychological characteristics, they too would succeed in the same fashion.

The third factor is available capital. Obviously, no investment is needed by those who present themselves

[4] St. Kitts uses the British West Indian dollar, which is the approximate equivalent of $0.58, U.S. currency.

for work on the estate, while to engage successfully in fishing requires substantial outlays for pots, nets and boats. I have estimated that it takes about $60-$75 B.W.I. to enter fishing with the required minimum of 5-7 pots. To amass this sum a man must save his money for months in advance. Many of the cane cutters complained that they could not become fishermen because the initial expense was too heavy. Yet most of the present fishermen were once estate laborers and managed to put money aside to buy pots. Therefore, we may conclude that what prevents other people from becoming fishermen is not so much the investment but the lack of the required psychological ability to plan ahead and save. Boats, too, are costly, but as two of the men who recently entered fishing paid $30 and $90 for their boats, this seems not to be an insuperable barrier. Furthermore, a man can always find a place in one of the existing crews and need not purchase a boat immediately. The problem all of the present fishermen face is a lack of co-workers to help man their own boats. One of the most striking indications of the lack of personnel is the large number of nets and boats in Dieppe Bay not presently in use. There are six gar nets in the village, and only enough men can be found to work three of them. There are sixteen boats beached on the sand, and only nine are in use. Of the other seven, three already have disintegrated for lack of care. There is, relatively speaking, an enormous surplus of equipment, but few men to take advantage of it.

Last, the income produced by the sea is at least as great as that which may be earned in the cane. Excluding very real benefits such as extra food, shorter working hours and a commodity with which to establish a basis for reciprocal favors, the income of the fishermen can be estimated at about $20 B.W.I. per week annually.[5] Many of these men, too, can reach heights of $40-$50 per week which is impossible on the estates.[6] The most successful fishermen earn as much or more as the managers of the

---

[5] Daily records of income were kept for a period of nine weeks.

[6] One fisherman's woman estimated that she spends, on the average, $37.50 in town for food each week.

estates; though, of course, they do not assume the same level of status.

However, the cane cutters tend to make less money in a longer work week. To estimate the income of the cane cutters I was able to get the weekly records from one man who was a young, strong and ambitious cutter working hard to save money to emigrate. He was, moreover, a head cutter, and so his wage during crop time included the extra dollar given for this special effort. His income, which is among the highest that cane cutters earned that year, showed an average weekly income of $15.59. His highest weekly wage was $29.70, which is much lower than the highest possible return in fishing.

Material possessions, too, give a good indication of income and reveal their relative standard of living. Approximately half of both groups own their own homes, with many more larger houses (over four rooms) being owned by fishermen. About a third of both groups have electricity in their houses and own a radio. Two-thirds are able to afford having a latrine in their yard. Finally, using livestock as a last measure of income, a larger percentage of fishermen own a substantial number of chickens (over six) and pigs (one or more) than cane cutters.

Since the market, ocean resources, available capital and income would all lead to the expectation that a much larger and more intense fishing industry should have developed in Dieppe Bay, I believe that we are forced to the conclusion that fishing, in its essential nature, demands psychological characteristics from its personnel that are in short supply on St. Kitts. Most individuals who have been reared under the conditions prevailing on St. Kitts either prefer to work on the estates or to emigrate. The distinction between Dieppe Bay and other fishing villages in the West Indies (see Chapter 8 for a discussion of a village of Jamaica) is that here a choice exists and, given this option, few decide to go into fishing. When no option exists, as in the above mentioned Jamaican village, the inhabitants are forced to engage themselves in fishing. Given this lack of option the nature of the fishing institutions that then develop are radically dissimilar to those present on St. Kitts. A detailed discussion of the personality of the fishermen in my sample, its causes and the way these men shape their work crews is presented in later chapters. It is sufficient at this point simply to indicate several of the psychological requirements of fishing which have made the choice so difficult for most Kittitians.

1. Saving

In order to enter fishing a man needs to own at least five to seven fish pots, with approximately 14 pots required to return the average fishermen's income. To purchase the raw materials he must be able to save about $130 to build these 14 pots. He will, moreover, need new pots every year, so saving is an essential aspect of his trade.

2. Withstand Losses

Fishing is a precarious business, not so much in regard to loss of life, although that threat is constantly present, but more in regard to loss of equipment. Boats get swamped or damaged by heavy seas, and fish pots suffer a constant process of attrition. People in Dieppe Bay are always speaking of the pots that get carried away by the sea or damaged in a storm. Every year each fisherman has to replace virtually all of his fish pots. Only a few of the residents of Dieppe Bay can bear these losses; the remainder do not become fishermen. The degree to which there is loss of fishpots can be estimated from the data in Table 3-2, which shows the number of fish pots owned by each fisherman in January when the season begins and new pots are set out, and October, near the end of the fishing year. It must be noted that the differential is not necessarily the extent of the total yearly loss, as men often replaced missing pots immediately.

3. Variable Income

In the cane fields the men know that they are guaranteed a wage for the work they do. Every time a man cuts a stalk of cane he knows he has earned a definite amount of money and that he will receive his wages regularly every Saturday afternoon. The fishermen, with no such assurance, must expend the same effort every time they go out, whether or not they catch any fish. Sometimes

TABLE 3-2

Fish pot losses

The Number of Pots in January	The Number of Pots in October
15	7
15	6
27	21
24	20
19	14
6	12
3	0
3	11
29	22
14	7
4	0
2	0
10	4
22	12
22	15
16	12
30	15
0	0
10	4
6	0

they can go for days or even weeks and find no fish in their traps or gar in the neighboring waters. But, although they must be able to withstand the uncertainty of their rate of income, the attraction of fishing is that occasionally they get an enormous haul. One fisherman speaks often of the day he caught $400 worth of fish, and during the months I was in the village there was one day when a gar boat returned with a catch that brought in $60 per man.

One last matter of concern are two major technological developments that have occurred in recent years. It has been the customary practice of these fishermen to use wooden longboats which they row out to the fishing grounds. In 1962 the government instituted a policy of stimulating fishing on an island-wide basis by offering loans for the purchase of engines. It was hoped that this would allow the fishermen to range farther from their home and intensify their activities, as well as attract more men into fishing. Although four men, including the two who had been using sails, had changed over to engines by 1963, there has been neither an increase of men interested in fishing nor any significant expansion of the work pattern. The second recent innovation was a shift from the use of cotton to nylon thread gar seines. The benefit of nylon is that it is sturdier than cotton and gets damaged much less easily. This means that the fishermen do not have to spend as much time tediously repairing their nets and therefore have more time for productive activity. However, although this, too, has been welcomed joyfully by the men already engaged in fishing, it does not seem to have brought about an increase in the number of men willing to man the gar boats.

4

The Personality Structure
of Cane Cutters and Fishermen

The personality structure of the fishermen and cane cutters might best be introduced by an admission of personal bias. During my first summer in the village, a time when I was not directly working on this project, I found myself enjoying the company of fishermen more than that of the cane cutters. I was continually struck by this fact while reviewing my notes and impressions after leaving the village. At first I feared that possibly my research of a few months time had been contaminated in some way I remained unaware of, but as I continued working through this material it seemed that favoritism, or personal likes and dislikes, are significant data which deserved scrutiny in their own right. After all, a field worker's responses to his informants are not due to mysterious whims, beyond our understanding. On the contrary, it is possible for these reactions to be most relevant and full of significance if their meanings are pursued. For this reason, it seemed important to examine why the men of different occupational groups should have produced different kinds of responses in me. And so, many experiences I had shared with these men during my general survey of the village took on new meaning and opened up an entirely new direction for the study of the village.

Perhaps most striking were the different receptions I received when I visited their homes. Often the cane cutters would invite me in, sometimes trembling both from unsureness of how to act and, possibly, pleasure at the enormity of my condescension. When I left, frequently there were hurried whisperings between the man and woman, and they might press some vegetables or eggs on me in gratitude for the visit. The fishermen, on the other hand, were much more matter-of-fact. They displayed more confidence in themselves as we spoke, and appeared much more to be evaluating me as a man, rather than as a representative of a seemingly superior culture. My initial impression was of a great difference in the degree of self-assurance between the two groups.

Their work, too, affected me differently. Fishermen seemed more daring and were involved in many types of labor. There was an element of uncertainty and excitement in their efforts—sometimes they caught much and other times nothing at all—but they seemed to face up to the vicissitudes of their life and expressed an enjoyment at the capriciousness of their trade. They emphasized that fishing was good because even though they might undergo long periods of failure, the thrill of the occasional large haul was adequate compensation. The cane cutters, however, spoke of how they were content to labor long in the fields because they knew that with every stalk of cane cut, money was earned. The difference between the groups appears in the fact that fishermen enjoyed, and seemed to demand, a variety of activities, with no supervision and control, and cutters accepted the unpleasantness of tedious unchanging work under strict supervision for the guarantee of a wage.

One of the most interesting contrasts which soon came to my attention was the way they behaved on their Saturday night spree. The fishermen did not seem to drink as much as the cutters, and when they felt themselves getting drunk often went home to sleep. During the time they drank the most noticeable quality was the laughing, joking, and good fellowship the rum seemed to bring out in them. Conviviality seemed to be the goal they sought from their spree. However, cane cutters seemed to be drinking more seriously and with greater desperation. Their purpose in drinking seemed primarily to be to achieve a state of drunkenness. There was much less vivacity in their actions and less contact with other people.

As I recalled my first experiences the cutters seemed more depressed about their life. They complained a good deal of the difficulties they faced and continually referred their problems to the mercies of their Lord. The fishermen were the only people in the village who spoke of pleasure in their work, and would call me to witness the beauties of their colorful fish, or the pattern of froth formed on the surface when a school of fish entered the harbor.

Of course, these were general impressions, for there were certainly convivial cane cutters as well as depressed fishermen. Yet, from experiences such as these it was possible to form general hypotheses about the psychological functioning of the men in each group, frame broad questions concerning their childhood experiences and design measures to determine the validity of the observed levels of personality.

In terms of Maslow's theory of the hierarchy of needs I felt that cane cutters were seeking goals on lower levels than fishermen. Specifically, cutters seemed to be functioning on the physiological and safety levels, while fishermen were on the higher levels of love and belongingness and of self-esteem. In order to explore these areas two major procedures were utilized. A number of questions were included in the Male Interview, given to all the members of my sample, that sought to determine if there was a divergence in their basic childhood experiences to which the observed difference in personality could be attributed. To achieve an objective measure of psychological functioning, a sentence completion test was constructed which focused on the areas pertinent to the personality theory used, and was given to all the members of the sample at a separate time.

I. BASIC CHILDHOOD EXPERIENCES

Events of great psychological magnitude must occur for one group of men to remain at the level of physiological and safety needs. It was therefore predicted that the cane cutters, relative to the fishermen, had undergone much greater instability in their basic childhood family experiences. For this reason three questions were asked on the Male Interview: the age at which the men lost or left their mother; the age at which they lost, or left, their father; and the number of their siblings who died while the men were still children. These areas were studied because the family in Dieppe Bay, as in most cultures, contains those people with whom the child forms his deepest affectional ties, and upon whom he relies for food and protection. As these bonds form the child's primary source of gratification, disruption of them results in grave deficiencies in his safety needs.

The experience of the cane cutters and fishermen in each of these areas was analyzed separately. Then, for each man, the three different events were examined together and a total score given to estimate his degree of satisfaction of the need for safety. It was felt necessary to consider the several factors at one time because the men had different degrees of loss in each relationship. For example, in some cases there was a moderately early loss of the parent but severe loss of siblings. In others, there was no loss of siblings but a very early loss of mother. As both types of loss produce severe deprivations of the safety needs, establishing a total safety deprivation score for each individual enables us to consider all experiences at one time.

1. The Number of Years with Mother

In Dieppe Bay, as elsewhere in the West Indies, the mother-child bond is of greatest importance. The mother has the primary responsibility for feeding the child, keeping him clean, looking after his health, socializing him, protecting him from other children, leading him into relationships with the total community, as well as serving as the richest source of love and protection any child is likely to receive. On the lips of most Kittitians I have met, and dramatized in loud and melancholy repetition in many calypsos, is proclaimed a deep and sentimental attachment for their mother as the person who cared most about them. When a child loses his mother, it is often said, he leaves his childhood and becomes a man.

There are several arrangements that usually follow the loss of one's mother. The child may be cared for by his maternal grandmother or else go to live with an aunt. Occasionally, he will be placed with a woman in the village who, though not a relative, takes pity on him. Seldom does he remain under his father's supervision. Of the forty men of my sample only three stayed with their fathers after their mothers died. This is due, in my sample at least, to the fact that at the time of the mother's death or emigration the father had either already left the family (the case of 26 of the men) or else had broken up the household (the experience of 11 men). Of these last 11 men, 9 at that time were already over 14 years old, and could earn money—and so had little call on their father's conscience or sense of responsibility.

It is important to realize, however, that although a woman does take the child in, she never can act as a total surrogate mother, lavishing all the care and affection the child was accustomed to receive. This is not surprising, for the woman who accepts the child is usually sufficiently harassed in her own right. In the case of the maternal grandmother the child comes under the care of one who is often an old woman, cranky, inflexible and subsisting on a meager income. If the child is given to an aunt it is usually true that she, herself, has a large family to provide for from her small means. Furthermore, as her own family is often large she cannot devote herself to the child. In any case, it is rare that another person has the same interest in a child as his own mother and is willing to give equal affection and protection. Sometimes these children fall into a Cinderella-like existence, are given all the household chores and suffer the persecutions of that woman's own children.

In sum, the loss of the mother has several lasting results. The shattering of the child's primary ties at an early age is a severe deprivation of the child's need for a stable world-orientation. The child loses belief in an ordered world and devotes much of his efforts to overcoming his sense of flux. He also tends to feel that forming affectional ties is dangerous because the person for whom he cares can suddenly leave him alone in the world. This leads him to the conclusion that people are untrustworthy, and to protect himself he closes himself off from further bonds with other people. This defense against the transitoriness of interpersonal bonds, as will be demonstrated shortly, characterizes the cane cutter, and has a great influence on the way he structures his interpersonal life. Moreover, the loss of mother removes the main source of love from his life and deprives him of his potentially most gratifying love relationship. Therefore, for one who has lost a mother early in life we may conclude that there has been grave deficiencies in the amount of love received. Another assumption we may safely make is that loss of mother also results in greater physiological deprivations, in both the areas of nutrition and medical attention. This conclusion is based simply on the fact that the average intact family in Dieppe Bay suffers from a poor diet and inadequate medical care. When the child is placed in another home the income his mother and/or father earned is not available, and he is an extra drain on the meager resources of those who now are attempting to care for him. Furthermore, he has a much smaller claim on whatever resources are available. We may conclude, therefore, that those men who have lost their mother early in life have had greater deprivation of their physiological needs and are now striving to gratify them as well.

The age of twelve has been used as an approximate limit of the age of significant childhood loss in this analysis and in several others, below, for the following reasons. Around the age of thirteen, children, in Dieppe Bay, are able to find work in various capacities; for example, cutting grass for the estate animals, helping out in the stores or assisting fishermen care for their boats. Further, around this age children become less involved with their families and spend most of their free time with groups of peers, ranging away from the village into the mountains or spearing fish along the coast.

Children younger than this, however, are much more dependent upon their families and spend a good deal of their time around the house helping their mothers with the household chores. In general, their deepest ties still seem to be centered in their family. For this reason, parental loss should be most disturbing to children younger than thirteen and less so to children who were older. Therefore, this age has been chosen as a rough measure indicating the degree of childhood loss experienced.

It must be realized, however, that the entire distribution of ages at the time of loss has been used in making intergroup comparisons, rather than simple judgments of above or below age twelve. The number of years the men in each group have spent with their mother is presented in Table 4-1. Each of the cane cutters is repre-

TABLE 4-1

Distribution of the number of years fishermen and cane
cutters spent with their mothers

	0	1	2	3	6	7	9	10	12	13	14	15	16	17	19	20	21	22	23	26	30	32	34	35
												F	F											
F				F			F		F	F		F	F	F	F	F	F	C	F	F	F	F	F	
C	C	C	C	C	C	C	C	C	C	C	C	C	C	C	C	C	C	F	C	C				C

Years with Mother

sented by the letter C, and each of the fishermen by the letter F.

Notable in this distribution is the fact that virtually all the fishermen have lived with their mother for thirteen years or more, the case for 16 of the 19 fishermen. Only one of the three other men has been a full-time fisherman all his life. The other two have just begun fishing the year of the study after having been forced out of their other lines of work by recent technological changes on the sugar estate. However, almost half of the cane cutters, 10 of 21 men, lost their mother before their thirteenth year. The Mann-Whitney U test shows a difference between the two groups in their age at losing mother at the 0.25 level.[1]

2. The Number of Years with Father

Although in the West Indies the primary figure in a child's life is the mother, presence or absence of the father is also an important factor. The experience of these men with their father does not show such marked differences as occurred with their mother. Yet there are important indications in the degree of contact with fathers which throws light on the contemporary personality of the two groups. Fourteen of the men (six fishermen and eight cutters) state that they never knew or lived with him. These results are difficult to interpret at this point because I have no exact information as to the arrangements their mother instituted after childbirth. Perhaps we should conclude that while the positive aspects of having a father were not present, such as increased economic support and a second major affectional figure, the negative aspects of a significant loss were also avoided. But of those who did possess their father after birth, the cane cutters show a much higher degree of early loss than do the fishermen. This distribution appears in Table 4-2.

Of those who had their fathers between the first year of life and the twelfth, six cane cutters and one fisherman suffered his loss: two losses through death and five through desertion. Virtually all the fishermen (12 of 13)

[1] All statistical analyses to be reported have been carried out with one-tailed tests.

TABLE 4-2

Distribution of the number of years fishermen and cane cutters spent with their fathers

0	1	2	6	12	13	14	15	17	18	19	20	21	23	25	26
F	F						C								
F	C						C								
F	C						F								
F	C						F								
F	C						F								
F					F	F		C	C	F	F	C	C	C	F
C		C	C	C	C	C		C	C	C	F	F	C	F	F
C			C	C							F	F			
C															
C															
C															
C															
C															
C															
C															

Years with Father

whose fathers remained with their mothers after their
birth retained possession beyond the thirteenth year. On
the other hand, 6 of 13 cutters lost their father before
their thirteenth year. Those who never lived with their
father perhaps had a more difficult life as their mother
was forced to assume the sole burden of support. But
they did not experience the shattering of affectional
bonds, which was the experience of six cane cutters. The
distribution in Table 4-2 shows a difference between the
two groups, excluding the men who never lived with their
fathers, at the .053 level, with the Mann-Whitney U
test. Loss of father is important to those men in the
sample who suffered the loss before their thirteenth year,
and is taken into consideration in arriving at the estimation of total loss which appears in Table 4-5, below.

3. The Loss of Siblings

Although the tie with the mother is the most important one in the child's life, bonds with siblings are also
of great significance. This is especially true in the West
Indies where the family is often very large and much of
the responsibility for the younger ones is turned over to
the older. In my sample, the family size ranged up to
18 children, with an average of 8.5 children. Also, because the mother must often work there is a further pressure to rely on the older children for the care, nurturing
and supervision of the younger (70% of these men report
their mothers had some kind of work.) During their
childhood their siblings often acted as parental figures,
and they, in turn, had to look after younger brothers and
sisters. In either case, they were thrown into close contact with their siblings and were forced to rely on them
heavily.

Because siblings formed such an important part of
their world, it is important to determine if there was a
differential in the degree of permanence of these relationships. For each group, I tabulated the number of siblings
who died while the men were still children. However, as
it seems likely that the loss of two siblings in a family
of four has a much more severe effect than the loss of
two siblings in a family of eighteen, the total number of
siblings was also tabulated, so that the degree of loss

incurred could be estimated. This tabulation is presented in Table 4-3. In this table, the "size of family" column

TABLE 4-3

The total number of children in the family, the number of live siblings and the number of sibling losses for fishermen and cane cutters

	Fishermen			Cane Cutters	
Size of Family	Number of Live Siblings	Losses	Size of Family	Number of Live Siblings	Losses
5	1	3	13	12	0
11	6	4	13	11	1
16	13	2	2	1	0
18	15	2	6	5	0
8	6	1	18	17	0
3	2	0	4	3	0
1	0	0	5	4	0
5	4	0	2	1	0
2	1	0	1	0	0
17	16	0	7	4	2
7	5	1	9	6	2
4	3	0	8	5	2
6	5	0	14	6	7
9	6	2	12	9	2
7	6	0	8	4	3
6	5	0	8	4	3
8	7	0	14	11	2
8	7	0	15	5	9
10	8	1	12	9	2
			15	5	9
			3	2	0

$\bar{X} = 7.94$ $\bar{X} = 6.1$ $\bar{X} = .84$ $\bar{X} = 9.00$ $\bar{X} = 5.9$ $\bar{X} = 2.1$

denotes all the children born into a family, including the subject, and a "live sibling" is defined as one present during the subject's childhood.

The size of the family for each group is approximately equal, 7.94 siblings for the fishermen and 9.00 siblings for the cane cutters. Therefore the differential in sibling losses cannot be attributed to a difference in family size.

Sibling losses, for the two groups, though, are very dissimilar in magnitude. The fishermen have experienced fewer deaths among their siblings; a group average of .84 deaths. Many have had no losses at all, and most have had only one loss or less; the case for 74% of the men. Only three men can be said to have had severe losses, for the losses of two siblings in families of 16 and 18 should be considered relatively moderate. On the other hand, the cane cutters are characterized by quite severe siblings losses; 52% of the cutters have experienced two or more deaths among their siblings. For the cutters the average loss is 2.1 siblings, which is 2½ times as great as the figure for the fishermen. The groups evidence a difference with the Mann-Whitney U test at the .085 level.[2]

4. Estimation of Total Loss

Both loss of parents and loss of siblings are effective in shattering the stability of a child's orientation, depriving him of love relationships and damaging his ability as an adult to form interpersonal ties. Because there are many instances where only one of these two main categories of loss occurred it is important to estimate, for each individual, the severity of all the safety deprivations suffered. Each case was analyzed separately, the several experiences considered, and then judged to have had either a high or low degree of childhood loss. A high/low scale was utilized as it is difficult to define with precision the specific factors involved in intermediate stages. In reaching this decision three criteria were utilized:

a. The age at which the child lost his mother.
b. The age at which the child lost his father.
c. The degree of sibling loss.

[2] It must be recognized that this analysis does not take into consideration the three cases (two fishermen and one cane cutter) who, though experiencing the loss of two siblings, still possessed large numbers of live siblings. The family size of these three men was 18, 16, and 14. If this judgment was included, there would be a larger difference between the two groups on the sibling loss dimension. This estimation will be made in section 4c below.

For the estimation of the loss of a parent, twelve years was used as an approximate limit of high loss. The death of one sibling in four during a man's childhood was considered an indication of high loss.[3] However, these figures were not applied completely arbitrarily. For example, in the case of one cane cutter who had lost his mother at the age of twelve, the fact that all of his 12 brothers and sisters survived his childhood was considered and he was scored as having a low loss. However, one whose mother died when he was ten was scored as high loss even though only two of his 11 siblings died.

After the severity of each individual's childhood loss experience had been estimated, the raw data was turned over to another judge to be rated independently, according to the three criteria.[4] In 39 of the 40 ratings the independent judge's estimations were identical with mine. In the one case of disagreement the independent judge's evaluation was, contrary to mine, in the predicted direction. The data and evaluations are given in Tables 4-4 and 4-5. In Table 4-6 the degree of loss for the two occupations is compared.

Summary

This analysis reveals clear-cut differences between the two groups. The cane cutters have suffered much greater instability and loss in their families and, therefore, have had severe deprivation of their safety needs. From these findings we are also able to infer that there has also been a much greater deprivation of the physiological needs.

The fishermen as a group have experienced less deprivation on the level of safety needs. Their families have been more stable and we may assume that, relative to the

[3] This ratio was decided on for two reasons. First, if the ratio was more than one in four it would indicate there were many other siblings with whom that man formed close attachments. Therefore, relatively speaking, much of his interpersonal ties remained intact. Second, in larger families there is the likelihood that the dead sibling was not very close in age, and so less of a bond was formed, which caused less effect when it was broken.

[4] Perhaps it is necessary to mention that the second judge knew neither the first estimations nor the occupation of each man.

TABLE 4-4

Parental loss, sibling loss, and estimated severity of total loss for cane cutters

Cutter	Size of Family	Number of Siblings Lost	Year Lost Mother	Year Lost Father	Severity of Loss
1	13	1	17	17	L
2	14	7	19	17	H
3	12	2	23	23	L
4	7	2	17	1	L
5	5	0	35	0	L
6	9	2	9	2	H
7	13	0	12	12	L
8	8	2	15	1	H
9	15	9	16	18	H
10	6	0	3	0	H
11	14	2	6	6	H
12	2	0	1	1	H
13	18	0	15	15	L
14	8	3	13	0	H
15	8	3	20	0	H
16	12	2	10	0	H
17	4	0	21	21	L
18	3	0	2	15	H
19	1	0	0	0	H
20	15	9	0	0	H
21	2	0	2	0	H

H = High loss
L = Low loss

cane cutters, they have received more gratification of their physiological needs. Further, the very stability of the significant relationships implies, all other things being equal, that they have received a greater degree of affection from their families. They should, therefore, be less mistrusting of other people, able to enjoy functioning on an interpersonal level and be more involved in searches for self-esteem.

II. PERSONALITY

In this section the findings on the personality structure of the fishermen and cane cutters, as determined by

TABLE 4-5

*Parental loss, sibling loss, and estimated severity
of total loss for fishermen*

Fisherman	Size of Family	Number of Siblings Lost	Year Lost Mother	Year Lost Father	Severity of Loss
1	9	2	22	19	L
2	4	0	30	25	L
3	8	1	26	26	L
4	11	4	14	14	H
5	5	3	34	0	H*
6	6	0	21	21	L
7	10	1	2	1	H
8	6	0	16	13	L
9	18	2	15	15	L
10	16	2	13	20	L
11	8	0	32	0	L
12	3	0	15	0	L
13	8	0	7	0	H
14	7	0	15	15	L
15	7	1	20	15	L
16	17	0	20	20	L
17	1	0	0	0	H
18	2	0	23	0	L
19	5	0	19	19	L

* This was the one case of disagreement. The second judge scored him as low loss.

a Sentence Completion Test, will be reported. The test was constructed to explore the various motivational levels described by A. H. Maslow and designed specifically to

TABLE 4-6

Severity of Loss and Occupation

	Severity of Loss	
	High	Low
Fishermen	5	14
Cane Cutters	14	7

$$X^2 = 4.99$$
$$p < .025$$

explore the categories of experience relevant to life in Dieppe Bay. For every need level all the completions in each protocol were examined for evidence of that need. Every statement on the protocol manifesting the need was counted, and a total was reached which was taken to reveal the strength of that particular need for that individual. Finally, the scores for each subject were compared in terms of occupational groups. In this way it was possible to compare the relative strength of the need and determine the predominant motivational orientation for each group. After I had scored the test, the protocols and instructions for evaluating the various levels were turned over to an independent judge. The correlation with his findings was extremely high and will be reported with the individual test results.

1. Physiological Needs

In the protocols gathered in Dieppe Bay, the physiological needs are manifested primarily in two areas. First, there were many responses dealing with matters in the broad category of food. These reflected states of hunger, concern for food or mention of related topics, like a "mother's breast." [5] The second group of responses covered the area of bodily integrity. Here were classified accidents, personal death and statements of bodily well-being.

Examination of the test protocols revealed, however, that the completions were not all of the same type. While many were clearly evidence of deprivation, others seemed to indicate that the issue was not of vital concern or that the individual had been gratified for that need. This qualitative difference led to a division of the above two categories into the dimensions of deprivation and satiation. Satiation responses, it was felt, demonstrate

[5] Much of the system utilized in scoring the Sentence Completion Test was adapted from the scoring manuals devised by David C. McClelland and his associates. These are published in *Motives in Fantasy, Action, and Society*, edited by John W. Atkinson (1958). In particular, in developing a method for scoring this need I derived much benefit from the article "The Effect of Different Intensities of the Hunger Drive on Thematic Apperception," by John W. Atkinson and David C. McClelland.

that the need is active; but, whereas deprivation responses give evidence that the individual has not been gratified in these goals, satiation responses indicate that the person is functioning on that level with, at least, partial satisfaction. This difference can be seen also as giving a rough intensity score; with deprivation responses indicating a strong motivational tendency and satiation responses indicating a lesser degree of need. The dichotomy into deprivation and satiation responses was especially strong in the areas of physiological needs and, therefore, was utilized only on this need level. One reason, perhaps, for the physiological satiation responses lies in the nature of the test itself. Many stems, on re-examination, seem to force the person being tested to produce completions dealing with these matters, e.g., "food is. . . ." This appears to be more the case for physiological needs than for the others. The following are the categories used to score the responses.

Food Deprivation. This is scored whenever there is reference to anything in the area of food. Hunger, eating, meals are all considered. For example, "I am hungry," "food is not so available," "my friend will give me something to eat," "my biggest worry . . . is my belly," ". . . looking for a friend, looking for something to eat."

Food Satiation. When there is a clear statement that the man has been fed, either presently or as a child, and is content with what he received it is considered a satiation response. For example, "When I was a child . . . nurse from my mother's breast," "Food . . . is good," "I feel happy when I eat," and "I like cold milk plenty." These all show that while food has relevance to their present need structure, there is no feeling of a desperate search.

Health Deprivation. This is scored whenever there is mention of pain or discomfort to the body, or if there is any kind of injury—either through accident or death. It is not counted if it is said that another person died or would die, as that might imply the loss of a loved one and therefore should, more properly, be scored on a higher level. Examples of these responses are, "I am tired," "hot," "sick," and "getting your eye digged out," "cut with whips," "lose my health and strength."

Health Satiation. This is scored when there is a sense of bodily well-being. It must be possible to infer that the subject feels in good health or is deriving some kind of pleasant sensations from his body. For example, "food . . . supports our bodies," "the best thing is to have good health and strength," "I am proud to know that I have my health," "I feel happy when I am sleeping."

Results. In Tables 4-7 and 4-8 are presented the distribution of the total physiological and the physiological deprivation responses, respectively. The satiation responses are not presented independently because of the relatively smaller number of the fishermen's physiological responses. Two cutters and one fisherman refused to continue after the first part of the test and were, therefore, dropped from the comparisons.

These results show clear-cut and significant differences between the two groups. Combining the total food and health scores, Table 4-7, demonstrates that physiological needs are much more of a concern for the cane cutters than for the fishermen. For the fishermen, 71% have only four or fewer completions in this area, while 73% of the cane cutters have five or more. Analysis of the distribution with the Mann-Whitney U test shows a difference at the .01 level of significance. The interjudge reliability, tested with the Spearman rank correlation, was .98.

Even more interesting are the relative differences in response frequencies in the various sub-categories. Approximately 78% of the cane cutters' responses are in the sub-categories of physiological deprivation, as compared to only 53% among the fishermen. For this reason a separate distribution was made contrasting the deprivation scores in the two groups, Table 4-8. This distribution reveals a difference beyond the .002 level of significance, with an interjudge reliability of .98. The assumption is that deprivation responses signify a lack of gratification of this need and a greater concern with achieving these goals. Satiation responses, on the other hand, reveal that although the individual is functioning on this level the matter is not of such desperate concern and does not dominate his motivational structure.

Clearly, if this assumption is correct, the two groups, as a whole, are functioning in very different ways. The

TABLE 4-7

*Frequency distribution of cane cutters' and fishermen's
total responses on the physiological level*

0	1	2	3	4	5	6	7	8	9	10	11	12	13	14	15
		F	F				F								
		F	F	F			F	C							
		F	F	F	F	C	C	C							
		C	C	C	C	C	C	C	F				C	C	C

The number of responses
F = one fisherman
C = one cane cutter

$p < .01$
(Mann-Whitney U test)

TABLE 4-8

Frequency distribution of cane cutters' and fishermen's physiological deprivation responses

	0	1	2	3	4	5	6	7	8	9	10	11	12	13
					F			C						
		F		F	F			C						
	F	F	F	C	C		C	C						
	C	C	C	C	C	C	C	C	F					
F	C	C	C	C	C	C	C	C	C	C	C	C	C	C

The number of responses

F = one fisherman
C = one cane cutter

$p < .002$
(Mann-Whitney U test)

total score shows that this need level is of great concern to the cane cutters and is of much less importance to the fishermen. The sharp contrast in the deprivation scores is a further indication that the cane cutters, as compared to the fishermen, are much more involved with finding gratification on the physiological level.

2. Safety Needs[6]

The childhood experiences of the cane cutters offer evidence of a great deal of instability and disorganization. We have seen that 14 of the 21 cutters have suffered a high degree of loss, either through the early loss of their parents or the loss of siblings. The childhood of the fishermen, in contrast, has been much more secure, for only 5 of 19 men have had a high loss, while the preponderance have had a low degree of loss. It was therefore felt that safety needs should be a dominant concern for the cane cutters, while for the fishermen safety gratifications should be of relatively less importance.

In scoring the Sentence Completion Test for evidence of safety motivation the following subcategories were used. Each subcategory taps different areas in which the constellation of safety gratifications are sought.

Reliance on External Authority. The mention of a protector, a stronger person or a set of rules to rely on indicates a lack of confidence in one's own powers and the need for an external power to order the world. All mentions of "God," "Lord," "Christ," "Master" were scored, as well as statements giving authority to others, e.g., "When they tell me I can't do it . . . might be good for me."

Untrustworthiness. In this category are scored statements showing that other people can not be relied on. For this to be scored there must be a clear indication that the trust with S is broken. Comments like, "I am proud of God, a friend who never changes," "my mother . . . played neglectful of me," "men . . . is so unjust

[6] The term "physiological," used to characterize the needs on the first level is, perhaps, misleading, as it implies that the other need levels are not organismically based. It is fundamental to this theory of personality to realize that all needs are considered based in the physiology of the organism.

that we don't know who to trust," "if a man envy me, make me lose my health and strength," "do not put trust upon anyone at all," reveal the unreliability of other people, as perceived by S, and are all scored.

Need Care. This is scored when there is the direct indication that care is desired. As before, the need for someone to look after S reveals his lack of confidence in his ability and his attempt to establish compensatory relationships. Examples of completions within this subcategory are; "A wife . . . take care of me," "A woman is good to me because they keep us clean and get our little supper and will protect it," "I have nobody to look after me," and "I want . . . care."

Reciprocity. This is scored when S tries to set up, or refers to, mechanisms which will ensure him aid, e.g., "I give them when I have it and they give me when they have it." There are other variations on this theme; mention of giving but not getting in return, giving in order to get and complaints that S has no friendships because he cannot give.

Loss of a Person. By this time the two groups of men should have had equal numbers of dead and missing relatives. These responses reflect the general uncertainty concerning the permanence of interpersonal ties. However, there must be no mention of affectionate feelings to the dead person, for those responses are scored under love needs.

Need Help or Advice. In many ways this is similar to the "Need Care" subcategory. It was differentiated in order to avoid the connotations of dependency and lack of self-reliance. What is sought by this subcategory is the desire for assistance in coping with life. Examples are: "A friend . . . if I need anything he does help me," "my father is not no help to me," "someone has died who was a help to me," "What kind of friend would you choose? 'Strictly someone who could help me.' "

Safety Gratification. This is scored when there is a clear indication that the safety needs have been gratified. "I was taken care of," "A friend is very kind to me" (the word "kind" means that the friend gives things that S likes), "I am glad to know that I have a friend to aid and assist me." This subcategory is used to show that at present there is safety, peace, protection and lack of danger. It is interesting to realize that this subcategory is not used too extensively in these protocols. This occurs because those people who feel secure tend to tell about the things that they do. Such statements are often interpreted as evidencing a sense of competence, and, therefore, are scored at the level of self-esteem.

Results. The scoring technique, as before, is to identify as many responses as possible in terms of the subcategories and then tabulate them in order to reach a total score, which is taken to indicate the strength of the safety needs for each individual. A comparison of the two occupational groups is presented by a frequency distribution in Table 4-9.

The two groups are clearly distinguishable on the level of safety needs. The frequency distribution shows that most of the fishermen make relatively few completions which reflect concern with these issues.[7] In contrast, hardly any of the cane cutters fall on the low side of the distribution, and all but one of the group have 9 or more statements dealing with problems of safety. Analyzing the results with a Mann-Whitney U test, the two groups show a significant difference beyond the .001 level, with an interjudge reliability of .99. Clearly, this demonstrates that cane cutters are highly motivated in the search for gratification of their safety needs. For the fishermen, this need level is not of such grave concern.

3. Love and Belongingness Needs

Positive Affiliative Statement.[8] This all-inclusive category is scored when there are comments indicating that

[7] The two categories of "need help" and "safety gratification" are, perhaps, equivalent to a "satiation" score, in that they both show a capacity to function on one's own. It is interesting that whereas these categories account for 33.9% of the fishermen's responses on this level, they only include 18.5% of the cane cutters' scores.

[8] For much of the rationale in establishing the scoring system for this need, I am indebted to the articles in the collection edited by Atkinson (*Ibid.*), "A Projective Measure of Need for Affiliation," by Thomas E. Shipley, Jr. and Joseph Veroff, and "A Scoring Manual for the Affiliation Motive," by Roger W. Heyns, Joseph Veroff and John W. Atkinson.

TABLE 4-9

Frequency distribution of the cane cutters' and fishermen's total responses on the safety level

0	1	2	3	4	5	6	7	8	9	10	11	12	13	14	15	16	17	18	19	20	21	22	23	24	25+ (25-36)
																							C	C	C
					C											C	C					C	C	C	C
F			F		F				C	C	C	C		C		F	F				F		C		
F	F		F	F	F	F	F	F	F	F	F	F	C	C	C	C	C		C	C					

The number of responses

p < .001
(Mann-Whitney U test)

a positive affective bond with another person exists, existed or is desired. There must be evidence of a warm companionate relationship. Bare statements of role relationships were not considered, e.g., "mother and son," "husband and wife." When this need is central to the motivational system there must be demonstration of feelings of belonging, being one of a group, and identification with group goals, as well as evidence of loving, being loved and being love-worthy. For example, completions which were scored for positive affiliative statements were: "A woman . . . is a companion," "A family . . . the whole relative [relationship] between father and mother," "I want . . . everyone to cooperate with each other," and "women . . . to love and cherish her."

If a captain or a head cane cutter stated that he took care of the men in some way, it was scored as a nurturant response. In general, any kind of nurturant comment was scored, e.g., "a younger woman . . . I should teach her something." Words like "among" and "with" are indicators of a shared experience and were also scored, e.g., "live with us," and "among my family." Relevant, as well, were direct expressions of affection shown for another. For example, in response to the stem, "When someone dies I," completions such as "mourn," "feel sad," and "grieve" were all scored.

This was also used when the completions indicated that something was being done together with another person, e.g., "We all meet together," "we will walk around together," "social life." But it is not scored when there is merely a description of a man's job, e.g., "A head cutter . . . leads a batch of men behind him when cutting cane." In this last example no interaction is evident.

Two general procedural points should be noted. Replies to the stem "I love . . ." were not scored because the key affective word is given in the test itself rather than by the subject, e.g. "I love . . . my neighbor." Yet, if there were special emphasis in the response it was considered that this emotion was being expressed: "I love . . . my children, very well, very well." Also, the word "friend" was not taken to mean the appearance of an affiliative need, because friends in Dieppe Bay tend to be defined in terms of the material benefit one may derive from them. Responses where this was clear were scored as safety needs. Of course by the term "friend" some may have meant to communicate a warm feeling toward another. Unfortunately, as this could not be determined in most cases, these responses were not scored on any level.

Results. The number of responses in the category of positive affiliative statements is an indication of the strength of the love and belongingness needs. I had hoped, in preparing the test, to include an estimation of the degree to which experiences on this level were considered unpleasant and retreat was sought by blocking, denials, clangs, perseverations, or negative statements. On some protocols these mechanisms were painfully clear, but as the overall reactions encompassed too many ambiguous responses that analysis, unfortunately, had to be omitted. A comparison of the results for the two groups is presented in a frequency distribution in Table 4-10.

TABLE 4-10

Frequency distribution of the cane cutters' and fishermen's responses on the love and belongingness level

C													
C						F							
C	C	F	F			F							
C	C	C	C	F	F	F	F						
C	C	C	C	C	C	F	C	F		F	F		F
0	1	2	3	4	5	6	7	8	9	10	11	12	13

The number of responses

$$p < .001$$
(Mann-Whitney U test)

For the first time in the scoring strong indications of the presence of a need are found among the fishermen, and the cane cutters shift to give relatively weak intensities on this level. Almost three quarters of the cutters have only two or fewer responses concerned with the love needs, while none of the fishermen produce so few. Half of the fishermen have seven or more responses, while only one cutter yields so many. Analyzing this distribution with the Mann-Whitney U test shows a significant difference beyond the .001 level, with an interjudge reliability correlation of .97.

The greater degree of concern with love needs manifested by the fishermen, as well as their ease of functioning on the interpersonal level, may be attributed to the greater degree to which they were fortunate in possessing stable families. All other things being equal, greater experience with those who are most likely to give love is evidence of having received increased gratification on this level. In this regard it is most important to note that the responses, assumed to reveal functioning on the level of love needs, deal primarily with the possession of, rather than demands for loving relationships. By this I mean that the dominant number of these responses were of the order "A woman . . . is a companion," rather than "I want . . . everybody to cooperate with each other." In other words, the character of the fishermen's responses shows acceptance and possession of these relationships, rather than desperate searches for these types of gratifications.

4. Self-Esteem Needs

The next level after love needs are the need for self-esteem and for the esteem of others. In scoring for the appearance of these needs one broad category was utilized. At the same time, examination of the protocols revealed many negative self-deprecatory comments. These attitudes are the precipitates of experiences in which the esteem needs have not been allowed to function. Therefore, a second category was created to record the degree to which the individuals studied possessed a negative self-image.

Positive Self-Esteem Statement. This is scored when there are feelings of self-reliance, self-acceptance, respect, power, competence, esteem, confidence, achievement, respectworthiness, prestige, leadership, autonomy, and dominance.[9] These motives portrayed on the test in many ways: "A father . . . comes first in everything," "A

---

[9] Maslow, *Motivation & Personality*, p. 120.

TABLE 4-11

Frequency distribution of the cane cutters' and fishermen's
responses on the esteem level

```
                  C   C
                  C   F
          C C C   F   F
          C C F   F   F
  C   C   C C F   F   F     C            F    F    F    F
  ┌─────────────────────────────────────────────────────
  0 1 2 3 4 5 6 7 8 9 10 11 12          14   15   18   20
```

The number of responses

$p < .001$
(Mann-Whitney U test)

wife . . . is the second in the home," "I am good at
. . . studying every little thing," "A woman younger
than me . . . is very good in its place," "I am proud
of the gift God give me so I could make a good living,"
"A grandmother . . . she was in front," "I am good at
. . . one and everything," "I would like to be a teacher
or settle in an office," "They is to show us respect,"
"When they tell me I can't do it I . . . make a trial—I
still make a trial," "Responsibility . . . in charge—fully
in charge," "I want . . . to live for some purpose before
time is expired."

Negative Self-Image. Often there are remarks deprecat-
ing one's own ability or revealing a lack of faith in one's
capacities. These are found in the negative comments, "I
was small and could do nothing," "I was a child without
sense," "When men curse . . . Me! I ain't bang my
mouth with them at all. The next thing I would be in
trouble," "When I am not treated right . . . I am sorry
to know I am not treated right. But what could I do,
think a great deal and said nothing at all." Some people
worry over their inability to support their family. Others
portray the world as hostile while there is nothing that
they can do about it.

Results. In Table 4-11 is presented a frequency distribution of the total responses dealing with the need for
esteem in both groups. The degree to which they possess
a negative self-image is contained in the comparison in
Table 4-12.

The frequency distribution presented in Table 4-11
provides positive evidence that the fishermen, as compared with the cane cutters, are strongly motivated on
the esteem level. The cutters' records are notable for the
paucity of responses in this area. Nine of the fifteen
cutters give three or fewer indications of a concern for
esteem gratifications. In contrast, all of the fishermen
produce four or more completions dealing with esteem
needs. On the basis of a Mann-Whitney U test this
demonstrates a significant difference between the two
groups beyond the .001 level of significance. The interjudge reliability correlation was .92.

Conversely, the cane cutters reveal a much stronger
degree of negative self-image than the fishermen. Ten of

TABLE 4-12

*Frequency distribution of negative self-image
among cane cutters and fishermen*

0	1	2	3	4	5	6	7	8	9
	F		C						
F	F		C						
F	F	F	C						
F	F	F	C	C					
F	F	F	C	C				C	C
F	C	C	C	C		F		C	C

The number of responses

$$p < .001$$
(Mann-Whitney U test)

the fishermen have none or only one completion which can be scored as evidence of feelings of self-disrespect. Yet fourteen cutters portrayed themselves in this way with two or more responses. This is a significant difference beyond the .001 level with the Mann-Whitney U test, with an interjudge reliability was .98. Here a methodological point must be noted. Negative self-imagery was only scored when there was a clear statement of self-belittlement. But, it must be realized that many of the completions which were scored as evidencing a need for safety assume a sense of personal inadequacy as their basis and might also have been included. If such an analysis had been understaken the size of the cane cutters scores would have been extremely high, indeed.

I have no data on childhood experiences which might have provided a measure of self-esteem gratification for the fishermen. However, it is clear from the sentence completion test that the fishermen are functioning on the esteem level. This can be predicted from our knowledge that they did, relatively speaking, receive gratification of their love needs. According to Maslow's theory, the gratification of the love needs automatically releases the higher needs of self-esteem. It may very well be true that their childhood was not one in which these needs were satisfied, because it is manifest from their behavior that an element of desperation has entered into the quest for esteem gratifications. This is evident in many of their responses centering on such issues as "in front," "comes first," "good in its place," and "in charge, fully in charge." We might conclude that this is perhaps a neurotic pressure, that their behavior in this regard is often inflexible and frequently harmful to their best interests. How the unrealistic form of this need manifests itself in their daily life is discussed at length in Chapter 7.

5. Self-Actualization

There was little in my experiences which encouraged me to feel that this was a meaningful dimension of life for the residents of Dieppe Bay. For the sake of a complete examination of the personality of the participants in the study, in terms of this theory, I wished to determine if any functioning on this level could be found. Scattered among the responses on the sentence completion test were a few remarks which one might conclude at least pointed in this direction. But the overwhelming mass of responses dealt with far different issues.

I had also included two questions on the Male Interview in hopes of exploring this level. The answers I received from this source conveyed a small indication of function and so deserve at least a brief mention. The questions were simple and extremely concrete: "What do you do when you are not working?" and "What do you like to do best?" The replies to both were examined as a unit and a rough decision was made as to whether or not that person presents some minimal indication of

TABLE 4-13

Presence of self-actualization in cane cutters and fishermen

	Self-Actualization	
	Some	None
Fishermen	9	4
Cane Cutters	3	9

$p < .05$
(Fisher test)

self-actualization. Comments such as "I like to raise birds," "I like to sing," "I like to go visiting," received a score. Their meaningfulness was seen especially in the light of many of the other answers, for example, "I remain neutral at home," "I rest off," "I go to my ground" [his small piece of cultivated land—in other words, he continues working]. These were seen as providing absolutely no evidence of self-actualization. A comparison of the two groups on this dimension is presented in Table 4-13.

This comparison should show that the fishermen as a group are functioning, at least to a very small degree, on the level of self-actualization, while for the cane cutters this self-actualization is almost entirely absent. For comparative purposes, both from the viewpoint of childhood experiences and contemporary social structure, this information may be used to reveal differences in the functioning between the two groups. For these purely theoretical reasons conclusions may be drawn from these data. I wish to state as strongly as possible that I am not claiming that the fishermen are a self-actualized group. Although there is a greater degree of expressive activity, as compared to the cane cutters, by an absolute measure the fishermen's statements are pitifully inadequate.

5

The Cane Gang

The sugar estate, as the basic maintenance system on St. Kitts, provides the proper place to investigate the power and limitations of psychological needs to structure economic organizations. Although it is a complex institution, which demands large-scale capital resources; managerial skills; island-wide coordination with the central factory; and international systems of regulation, price setting and distribution, within this framework the structuring of work group organizations by the laborers remains a relatively autonomous process. In this chapter I shall analyze, in detail, the structure and functioning of the cane cutting gang and explore the relationship of its form to the dominant needs of the cutters. In Chapter 6, I shall present the variations of this organization which have developed on other West Indian islands in order to show the spectrum of diversity possible, within the same general institution.

I. RECRUITMENT, TRAINING, AND FORMATION OF THE GANG

As the village child matures and begins to decide on a course of life, he is confronted with three major alternatives. He can attempt to achieve middle-class status through success in school, followed by a job in one of the activities which serve the sugar industry. He can focus his goals outside the island and, usually with the help of a close relative, plan to leave the village for England or the United States as soon as possible. Last, he can seek employment on the estate, in one of several capacities. For most of the boys who grow up in the village, estate work is all that is available.

If he is going to work on the estate, around his sixteenth year he will present himself to the manager and ask for a job. At this stage he is willing to accept whatever chore happens to need a laborer. Usually he will work at one of the many daily tasks required at various times in the year. He might, for example, work around the estate house, or in the yard looking after the livestock. Alternatively, a beginner's work in the cane might involve carrying water to the men in the fields, or joining a "day-work" gang, composed of boys and old men, and spending several years hoeing, weeding, and planting the fields.

From these poorly paid odd jobs the boy eventually gravitates into one of the main adult occupations. Among these are permanent jobs caring for the animals, operating the brakes on the cane carts (which offers the hope of eventually becoming a tractor driver) or cutting cane. In the past, positions in the field loading cane into carts ("handing") and packing the cane at the railroad siding into small railroad cars ("packing") were available. Because of technological developments these activities are no longer present.

Those who have decided, or have been asked by the estate management, to become cane cutters learn the trade in one of two ways. Some will have picked up the rudiments by watching older friends cut cane and occasionally helping them out for fun. Most enter a boys' gang for a year or so and cut cane in a more relaxed atmosphere while they practice their skills. These gangs are not under great pressure and the boys get paid a flat rate by the day. After a period of time in these gangs, they are placed in the main cutting gangs, as positions become available.

By the age of sixteen many boys are forced to assume much of the responsibility for themselves and their families. This is especially true when their father is not present in the household. It is an even more urgent necessity if their childhood was spent in a relative's care. From a psychological point of view, in many ways this work is quite appropriate to their needs and capacities. They receive money each week, which they use to contribute to their families and provide themselves with the pleasures and profligacies of the man's world they are entering. If the fancy strikes, they need not be obliged to show up for work on a particular day and they need assume little responsibility for, or great commitment to, their work.

The answers the cane cutters gave to the question on the Male Interview, "Why did you choose cutting," reflect their lack of life chances and the simple urgency of the needs they wish to satisfy. The following is a sample of their responses.

"Find I can make a piece of living in it."
"Nothing else for me to do on the estate but that."
"Couldn't get no other kind of work."
"They were short of cutters."
"Make more money than in daywork."
"Money was small in carrying water."
"Rather to cut—more easier job than packing—not many jobs here in Dieppe Bay."

How the men feel about their present work was amply revealed by the question, "Do you prefer fishing or cane cutting?" Whereas all the fishermen insisted that their trade was best, only half of the cutters stated that they preferred cane cutting. The manner in which the two groups answered this question was also significant. Cutters responded by discussing the drawbacks of fishing, if they preferred cutting. If they felt cutting was less preferable, they spoke of the lack of funds to enter the fishing trade. Significantly, no cutters spoke of the advantages of cutting. In comparison, all the fishermen vociferously expounded the benefits of a fishing life. In their choice of reasons for not attempting fishing, the cutters present some of their main orientations to work. They claim that fishing is too

(1) *unpredictable:* "Fishing is too uncertain—have to hold up too long to get a penny."
"In fishing don't mean that every day you catching fish. But in cane—every day it's there."
(2) *dangerous:* "No tree to hold on to—no way to escape."
(3) *requires saving:* "Can't save enough money to buy pots —would rather be at the bay."

Fearing these aspects of the fishing trade, cane cutters turn their backs on the only possible alternative occupation in the village and continue their life in the cane.

Most cutters entered the cane early in life and have never engaged in other work. The median age for beginning work is twenty-two years. Of the 21 men in the sample, 12 have never held other jobs at all. Four worked previously at handing cane or at day work on the estate, for a brief period. Two were packers for most of their lives and started to cut only after they were injured. Only three of the men did other work—as a sailor, a government laborer, and a sharecropper on a neighboring island. This pattern is quite dissimilar from the one which obtains in fishing, and its implications will be discussed further in Chapter 7.

The enfolding sugar estates attract laborers from neighboring islands as well as from nearby villages. Because of its relative wealth and abundance of jobs, St. Kitts historically has been the goal of men from poorer islands seeking work. At present only four of the 21 cane cutters residing in Dieppe Bay were actually born in the village. Six were born in neighboring villages. Eleven men, 52% of the total resident cane cutting force of Dieppe Bay, were born on other islands; which is a fact of great importance for understanding the subculture of the cane cutters. They are drawn predominantly from Nevis, which is only one hour from St. Kitts by daily launch, while the rest came from the nearby islands of Montserrat and Anguilla. These men, similar to the native cutters in distribution of loss in childhood, assume the added burden of psychological insecurity which accrues from migration. (See p. 170 for a discussion of the psychological effects of migration.)

II. STRUCTURE OF THE GANG

As one enters the fields from the dirt tractor path leading up from the village, it is evident that the men who cut cane are organized in a definite pattern. The observer notices clusters of men, nine to eleven in number, in different sections of the field. The cutters are strung out in a line against the sugar cane with one end deeper into the field than the other. It is as if the men were a wedge which is being driven into the field.

Each cutter stands two rows apart from his neighbor

and works with a steady rhythm. He cuts the stalk near the base with his machete, strips off the leaves, cuts the cane in two and tosses the pieces onto a pile. As he penetrates deeper into the field, he leaves piles of cut cane behind him at regular intervals.

In each field, serving all groups of cutters, is a mechanical device for loading the cane into carts. This device, known variously as the "iron man," "grab" or "Broussarder" (after the manufacturer), is essentially a tractor with a mechanical claw. When a number of piles of cut cane have been laid down, the "Broussarder" lumbers over to the group of men, grabs a mound of cane with its claw and places it into the cart. It combines, without distinction, cane cut by all the men of a particular group. Tractors, dragging two carts, then take the cane to the railroad siding where it is placed into railroad cars and sent to the factory.

Mixing the cane from all the men in a gang has great significance because it ensures that their labor is rewarded by the achievement of the group as a whole and not by their efforts as individuals. Briefly, the method of payment is as follows. The cane is taken to the railroad line and transported to the factory where it is weighed. That weight of cane is credited to the gang, and whatever tonnage is cut during the week is divided among the men. The individual's share, calculated by the number of days he has worked, is paid to him by the estate on Saturday.

A system of payment based on the total group's effort leaves little room for individual achievement. It is impossible for a person to decide, by himself, that on a given day or week he will cut more cane, because the pattern of cutting arranges and regulates the speed at which each man works. Every person must remain a fixed distance behind the cutter on his right and in front of the one on his left, and forging ahead would disrupt the rhythm of the group. Even if an individual cutter could cut more on a given day, the system of payment is such that he could not benefit exclusively, but would only be augmenting the income of his slower fellows.

However, inversely, a system that demands that the men work together is also one which does not require a cutter to perform as an individual. There are several advantages that this group system holds out to the cane cutters. First, by participating in a gang, the men need not assume responsibility for the work. This is the function of one cutter designated by the estate to lead the gang. Called the "head cutter," he always takes up the first row to start the cutting for the day. His role in the gang will be discussed in the next section. Here it is sufficient to mention that he assumes responsibility for what the gang is to achieve and, in general, functions as a taskmaster. The men feel that if they worked alone, with no one to push or haul them along, there would be the ever-present danger that their pace would slow down or that they might stop work altogether. Working in a gang of men, "ruled," as they term it, by a head cutter, they need not assume the responsibility for their efforts and still can get the work done, which they must complete to survive.

A second benefit of group work claimed by the cane cutters, is the possibility of doing a little less when they are tired or ill. If they worked alone they would lose a good deal of money the day they were sick. Since they are working as a group at those times, they would be helped by sharing what the other men have cut for the day.

The third benefit gained by working in a large gang is the support they gain from one another in that the men continually make jokes, which encourages them all to work. Although not an instance of the mythical happy slave, laboring joyfully under the hot sun, the atmosphere of the large gang is nevertheless somewhat pleasant. The men are close enough to exchange stories, poke fun at someone, curse the estate or sing snatches of the latest calypso to each other. This interchange lets them feel, as they say, more "comfortable" and makes an exhausting and boring job more bearable. Furthermore, the men feel that if they were working alone they might be tempted to leave work early. In the gang, there are always a few men who will be feeling good at that time and who would say "let's go ahead" when they would be ready to quit. Because of the gang structure, the men are encouraged by the rest to stay, and so more likely to bring home money.

The validity of this last point is seen whenever only three or four of the eleven men show up for work. Monday is often a day when few men turn out because the others are still affected by the weekend spree. Usually, those men who do show up do not work strenuously and leave the field early. This also occurred several times during my stay on other days of the week, with the same result. The men either idled along for a few hours before going home or else decided there were not enough men to cut and did not even begin. This shows their reliance on, and need for, the total gang. If they had even worked slowly for just a few hours they would have been credited with a full day's work—which ultimately would have been taken from the cane cut by that day's absentees later on in the week.

Although the reaping of sugar cane on St. Kitts utilizes the structure of the large gang, it must be clearly understood that it is not a highly integrated unit with great solidarity. Rather, the reverse is true. The men have been placed together by the estate manager under the leadership of a head cutter who is selected by the estate. The structure of the cane gang shows a great cleavage between the head cutter's position and the men's, and few functional ties and little solidarity exist between the cutters. Essentially, the structure of the gang is a series of separate dyadic relationships between each of the men and the head cutter.

This structure is evident in those activities of the gang which lead to unresolved conflict and feelings of injustice. One large category of complaints the cutters raise against the head cutter arises from the nature of the contoured field, where the rows of cane to be cut are not all the same length. Frequently, there are perhaps a dozen very short rows at the beginning of the field, lengthening out to long rows of approximately equal extent and closing with another series of progressively shorter rows. What often happens is that the head cutter and the next two or three men, who are the strongest and fastest workers, get to cut very short rows of cane. By the time the fifth through eleventh man begins to cut, the rows have gotten much longer. The difficulty comes from the fact that, as they reckon it, all rows are counted as equal. This means that many of the men are doing much more work than the head cutter for the same pay. As one of the cutters responded on the Sentence Completion Test to the stem, "A Head Cutter":

A head cutter is to [take] advantage [of] you. He will cut four bunches of cane or a half a row, when you, which is the other man, behind him has to cut a row and a half, or two rows more than he. And if you do not cut out your row you still cannot earn your day's work. He still goes to the management and take a half a day from you [when] he hasn't cut even a half row.

A potential remedy for this grievance would be for the men to get together and, working as a unit rather than as individuals following their own clearly demarcated rows, cut out all the short rows at the beginning and end of the field. But they do not unite in this way and instead, resign themselves to an injustice which reappears weekly. This failure to utilize a potential mode of cooperation epitomizes the group's atomistic structure. The reason for this lack of unity, for even a brief period, lies in the mistrust each cutter entertains of his fellow workers. They are simply suspicious of the effort the other men would make in a joint operation and expect them to slack off, to "skulk" as they put it, at tasks in which responsibility is not clearly defined.

This attitude was clearly revealed on the Sentence Completion Test. Generally speaking, the cutters did not show much ability to respond to others or a desire to enter into close contact. In their completions to the stem, "men," for example, they presented a picture of a group who were suspicious of people's attitudes to them, responding with sentences such as "men . . . is so unjust that we don't know who to trust," and "some men heart is dark." [1]

As work progresses through the day, matters continually arise which show us the structure of the group as well as the sources of strain. For example, decisions must be reached concerning the amount of cane to be cut during the day; the speed at which work will proceed; when to

---

[1] See p. 133 for a group comparison with fishermen.

cease cutting; whether to make one long cutting or to cut for the morning, break at mid-day and return to the fields in the afternoon for a second time; and who shall represent the cutters to the union and management when disputes arise. In all these matters decision is left in the hands of the head cutter. That the head cutter does not unselfishly concern himself with the needs of the men, or, indeed, scrupulously refrain from satisfying himself at their expense, is seen in the response another one of the cutters gave to the stem, "A Head Cutter." His resentment is evident. After complaining that the head cutter takes the short rows and leaves him the long, he continues:

> . . . The next thing he's doing he doesn't let anyone know when he is making one work. We are working like a fool. He tells you to walk without a bread and his breakfast coming. So he eats his lunch—he cools off while we are working—and gone back in to work. And he worked us to 3 o'clock without nothing to eat.

And the reaction of his gang to this treatment? This he tells us in the next response to the stem. "Men." He exclaims, "men who are working with him do not told him nothing about it."

One wonders why the men do not exert pressure to change this arrangement. The power to take advantage of the men is in the head cutter's hands, but the system upon which it is based has not been determined by the estate management. In general, the estate merely places eleven men together, designates one as head cutter and leaves it to them to work out the internal arrangements. As long as the gang is working and the day's quota is being met, the manager will not meddle into the gang's affairs. If the men complained or disrupted the reaping process, then the manager would speak to the head cutter and make him change his ways, because he needs the men more than the head cutter. Therefore, the men have the power to dismiss the head cutter at any time by exerting their solidarity and refusing to work with him. In broad terms, the gang could function anywhere along a dimension from authoritarian to democratic or from atomistic to integrated, and the decision is strictly up to the men. Many times each year the crucial question of relationship between the head cutter and the men arises. Invariably, the decision is made to return to the series of isolated dyadic bonds between the men and the head cutter.

This internal structure rests, I submit, in the nature of the psychological needs of the cutters themselves. It is not that the men bear the injustice silently. On the contrary, one observes an enormous resentment in the men toward the head cutter, manifested by a continual stream of complaints and abuse. As one of the men, who had himself once briefly been a head cutter, remarked, "sometime so much abuse make you mother come back alive." The men do express such feelings toward the head cutter who generally regards it as part of his job and attempts to bear up tolerantly under the strain. But the men do not make an issue over their grievances or provoke a clash with the head cutter. This is the crucial psychological fact at the heart of the gang structure. As we have seen in Chapter 4, the cane cutter is not one to release emotion directly. Having experienced the dangers of this mode of experience so fully in childhood, he fears forming ties or confronting another directly. Instead, he tends to withdraw from a threatened clash, as he tends to withdraw from all significant human bonds.[2]

On the projective test there was a question designed to reveal the cane cutters' reactions to an act of justice: "What happens if the man over you doesn't treat you right?" A few men attempted to change the situation in some way, or to retaliate against the one who caused the wrong. For example, some men responded by stating:

"I leave him."
"I wouldn't feel satisfied and I would quarrel over it."
"I will go to my representative and put the matter to him. And they would come to him and they would have to say something to him. To keep down botheration."

However, most of the cane cutters' reactions revealed a

[2] See pp. 134ff for a discussion of the cane cutter's and fishermen's ability to confront other people directly.

thoroughgoing passivity. Often they felt a sense of hope-lessness and could only express their pain. Few of the cutters did more than signify the lack of trust they had in their own capacities. This is extremely important be-cause the reality of the cane gang is such that, if con-fidence rather than fear in their powers of action was felt by the men, they would challenge the head cutter. Eleven of fifteen cane cutters answered with such pas-sive responses as given below. See Table 7-10 for a com-parison with the fishermen's responses to this question.

> "Leave it in the care of God. He will find it out for himself."
> "I am sorry to know I am not treated right, but what I could do. Think a great deal and said nothing at all."
> "My heart will be hurted."
> "I cannot keep well."

In summary, because it is necessary to throw together large numbers of individuals who are often strangers to the village (see chapter seven for a discussion of psycho-logical "strangers") and who are generally functioning on the level of frustrated safety needs, a psychological imperative for non-integration is created. This precludes the possibility for cooperation among the men and forces them into dyadic relationships with the head cutter and the estate. A cooperative structure can only come into being when there is at least a minimum level of trust and affiliation among the workers.

The structure of the gang as it is constituted on St. Kitts is not the only possible method of reaping sugar cane—the inexorable product of the large-scale business-oriented sugar estate. Conceptually, there are a number of ways cane might be cut, and in the next chapter I shall present some of the types which have developed on other West Indian islands. For example, cane might be cut individually; by two men; by small groups; large gangs; large gangs which remunerate the men for what each reaps individually; families; etc. That the cane gang structure develops in this way can only be attributed to the organization these men must have in order to func-tion best. To this extent, it is proper to conclude that the specific form created is the result of the psychological needs of the individual cutters.

A Further Development on St. Kitts:
The "Broken Gang"

A recent development on the estates surrounding Dieppe Bay contributes to our understanding of the underlying dynamics of gang structure. In the last few years there were several cases of cane gangs having conflicts, too great either to be resolved or ignored, which led to their fragmentation.[3] The men refused to work with each other or with the head cutter, broke up, and went their separate ways. Sometimes alone, and in two's, three's and four's, as they chose, they continued cutting in the absence of the large gang for the rest of the season. Most important, each of these "broken gangs" worked at their own pace and under their own direction and the men assumed complete responsibility for the entire range of their individual efforts. The mechanical loader waited until they had cut enough to fill the two carts, that were especially designated to hold each man's tonnage. As this amount of cane is just the capacity of a railroad car, working without the entire gang did not produce any dislocation in the system of moving the cut cane to the factory. This experience with "broken gangs" demonstrates three points which are crucial to the general argument. The advent of the "broken gang" shows that it is possible both to challenge the head cutter's authority and to cut sugar cane on St. Kitts in organizations other than the large gang. Also, during this period, according to the estate manager, the estate worked just as efficiently as before. We may conclude, therefore, that the large gang is not an inevitable form on St. Kitts, linked to the effective functioning of a modern sugar industry.

Serious arguments between the men in these gangs, or between the men and the head cutter, culminating in a substantial rearrangement, is a much different way of handling conflict. For the cutters, entering into a clash of this kind necessitates exposing themselves to a human relationship to a much richer degree than before, and they must react at a higher level of personality. With-

[3] Few of the men in my sample were in these gangs.

drawal and submission on the one hand, and confrontation and attack on the other, are very different states of personality. When men feel that they cannot work together any longer and split up into one to four man units, a development of major psychological magnitude has occurred. These men are no longer laboring as isolates under the control and guidance of a self-imposed external power. They have demonstrated, by this action, a need to fight injustice; an ability to maintain contact with other individuals over an extended period; a capacity to work cooperatively as a small unit; and, perhaps even more important, they have assumed command of their persons and responsibility for their efforts. They no longer need a head cutter to act as taskmaster, nor do they wish to hide behind a group effort.

Significantly, the gangs that broke up were those composed of men who were born in the area of the estates. Those gangs which contained a mixture of men born outside of St. Kitts plus some from St. Kitts remained intact. In 1962, on the neighboring estate, two of the three cutting gangs broke up. The one that did not break up was composed mostly of men drawn from Nevis and Anguilla. We may relate this change in psychological functioning to two causes. First, because the gangs that did break up were composed of men born in the area, their members did not suffer the extra insecurity brought on by being a stranger in a hostile environment. In such an environment strangers huddle together for the security of numbers and the chance to shield themselves from the glare of public recognition. Second, as evidenced in the declining infant mortality and adult death rate,[4] Dieppe Bay, and St. Kitts as a whole, is becoming a safer place to live. Major diseases and epidemics have been curbed; the estate workers have achieved a relatively steep rise in pay in the last twenty years—due to the efforts of the union, resulting in more food and generally better living conditions; and, the union has taken over the government, so they feel exploited by one agency less. This has

[4] In the period between 1919-1931 the infant mortality rate (the ratio of deaths under one year per 1,000 live births) averaged 233, and the death rate was 27 per 1,000 people. By 1948, the figures were 99 and 15, respectively (Kuczynski, 1953).

led, I believe, to an increase in the degree of security, with a concomitant release of higher psychological energies. In the one gang that did not fragment, there was one person who did break away to cut by himself for the remainder of the year. He was a young man, born in the area, with a history of extremely secure family ties, as I have measured security. He lived at home with both of his parents until the age of seventeen; and of his twelve siblings only one died. He fancies himself a calypsonian and is the idol of many village boys who sing his scurrilous reflections on village affairs.

When the break-up occurs in the cutting gang, as it does with incredible frequency among the fishing crews (which will be discussed in Chapter 7), the cutters individually and as a group forsake the security offered by the large gang. These arguments and fissions should be seen as great advances in their need and capacity for interpersonal relationships and in their desire for self-esteem. That eventually the cutters returned to the pattern of subordination and non-responsibility of the large cutting gang is a major indication of the strength of the need for security among these men, and the difficulty they have in functioning on higher levels.

The recent occurrence of "broken gangs" is an event of major theoretical importance. Whereas most of the ethnography concerns stable institutions, this development allows for the investigation of a structure which is, perhaps, in the process of being formed. Looked at in this way, the "broken gang" can be seen as an ongoing naturalistic experiment in which the cause and effect relationship between psychological and social determinants can be easily understood.

ROLES

The psychological forces, that produce the position of head cutter and isolate it from the other positions in the gang, charge the man who occupies that position with many special tasks and obligations. In the previous section we have examined the relationship between these positions. Now we must explore the required duties and understand the gratifications the men demand from each other. The nature of the roles found in the cane cutting gang are the conditions by which these needs are met.

Dominating the motivational system of most cane cutters is the desire for a safe, stable and highly organized world. On the estate, they feel that they can achieve security and escape job requirements demanding a sense of competence and initiative: all of which are thrown into the hands of the head cutter, who must organize the group, provide the energy for its continuation and assume the entire range of responsibilities required for its functioning. Most of the duties seen as the head cutter's role, and the lack of duties seen as the obligations of the men, may be attributed to this basic process.

I shall discuss four aspects of their roles. First, the specific duties which fall in the head cutter's province. Second, the necessity to set the pace and give "encouragement." Third, the qualities of tolerance and forbearance demanded by the men under their complaints and cursing. Fourth, the process determining the basis of respect which accrues to each role.

1. Duties of the Head Cutter

At the beginning of the crop the head cutter decides on the position each man is to take in the gang for the rest of the season. In theory the men in the first few positions are supposed to be the best workers, but as the gang, in practice, works at the same rate, the head cutter is able to order the men according to his own desires—a decision that has important implications for the rest of the gang. When work starts in the morning the head cutter is always the first to begin cutting. After he has been cutting for approximately ten minutes and has advanced a short distance into the cane, the second man starts work on his row, followed, after a time, by the third man, and so on throughout the gang. The men never confront the cane as a group nor commence work at the same time. One result of this pattern is that those men in the gang's first positions finish their tasks earlier and are often able to avoid spending the hottest part of the day in the fields. Also, if the field is contoured, they may get to cut much shorter rows. Favoritism, as well as a desire to work beside personal friends, plays a large part in the head cutter's choice of internal order, against which the rest of the men exert little influence.

After the head cutter organizes the gang, one of his most important duties is to keep track of the number of days worked by each man, assign him his proper share in the week's output, and convey this information to the estate manager who makes up the weekly payroll. This is necessary because not all the men come to work each day or always labor for the entire day. If a man reaches the field in mid-morning he cannot cut as much cane as those who have been there since dawn. Sometimes the amount of cane cut by the men working the whole day is just too great to make up by working on after the rest go home, even assuming the late-comer wanted to work without the presence of the gang. Occasionally, too, a man falls ill during the course of the day's work, or has to return home for personal reasons. All of these variations in length of time worked by the men must be balanced off against the amount of cane they cut. Otherwise, since the output of cane is calculated on the basis of gang and not by the individual, there would be the ever present invitation to shirk the amount of work required of him. Since these men do not have the ability to see the cutting as a group enterprise, this presents a very real danger. This problem is met by calculating each man's contribution to the total output by the length of time he spent in the fields—measured in terms of the "day." A man, then, receives a share of the output proportional to the number of "days," or their fraction, that he worked.

Another of his duties is to supervise the quality of the work. For example, the cane should be cut close to the root and not too much stalk should be removed when the cutter chops off the green leafy head. The cutter also must take care to strip off the leafy covering (the trash) as well as make sure that little trash is mixed in with the cane on the piles he makes for the mechanical loader. All these acts, in this system, must be regulated or else the cutters will relax their care.

As the head cutter is the first one to cut each day, as well as generally being the fastest worker, he is frequently a good deal ahead of the gang. When this happens he stops work for a rest during which time he surveys the gang's efforts. This usually consists of a relaxed sweep of the eye while joking with the men who are still working. If the cane is being cut in a deficient manner he will, ordinarily, point out the shortcomings to the cutter and ask him to take more care. If a good deal of cane has been cut poorly, the head cutter may ask the man to go back over the work and set it right. On this issue the head cutter has a good deal of power, for if the man refuses to correct what the head cutter sees as faulty labor, he can estimate the time it takes to cut that cane and withhold that amount—measured as fractions of a day—from a man's pay. He will then set another of the cutters to work on the section under contention and pay him with the amount deducted from the first cutter's wage.

One of the most frequent complaints heard against the head cutter is the disparity between the magnitude of work left undone and the amount of money withheld and given to another cutter. Further, it is claimed that he has favorites in the gang to whom he bestows these plums; which is still another reason to be on good terms with him. Running through many of the protocols, and as an admitted fact in many personal conversations, was the recognition that these remedial steps were often fully deserved. For example, on the Male Interview men stated:

"[head cutter is responsible]. . . to see work done. Search row and see if it is properly done. If not get another man and the pay comes out of your salary."

"Some people don't do the amount of work and, [therefore], don't get the amount of pay like the rest."

Generally speaking, these men were quite consciously aware that they would often do poor work. When caught they fully expected to be punished, though they might argue that the punishment was too severe. Yet they do not seem to bear guilt for their shortcomings or to assume responsibility for the quality of their efforts. All that is placed squarely in the care of the head cutter.

The needs that impel the cutters to structure the gang, create the position of head cutter and transfer the regulatory mechanisms from themselves to the head cutter, make of that position the key link between the men and the larger estate organization. Virtually all communication between them takes place through the agency of the head cutter. Decisions reached by the estate manager as to when cutting will proceed; the specific field to be cut; changes in work practices and evaluation of the speed and quality of the labor are given to the head cutter. It is he who passes on the instructions to the men because it is he who has the obligation to see that the estate's decisions are carried out. The estate sees little point in going directly to the men when neither the manager nor the men themselves are going to assume the responsibility. At the same time many of the immediate difficulties that arise among the cutters go directly to the head cutter instead of to the estate manager. For example, whenever quarrels arise it is the head cutter who is expected to smooth them out. Injuries to the men in the course of the work, as well as illnesses of a more general nature, are deemed to be part of the head cutter's role and are not brought directly to the attention of the manager. It will only be the most extreme provocation, such as a credible threat to poison a fellow worker, that will go to the estate manager. And then, too, the head cutter is directly involved.

Other difficulties, such as complaints of bad conditions in the fields, which are occasionally overrun with weeds, vines, and guinea grass due to carelessness on the part of the management in tending the growing fields of cane, are frequent occurrences. These, as well, are not taken directly to the management by the men. Rather, the cutters expect the head cutter to present their grievances and bargain for a work premium. This occurs even though the head cutter can be seen as the lowest rung of the estate bureaucracy and the union representative continually reminds them that they have an official to carry out that function. Nevertheless, the men have transferred so much of their efforts to the head cutter, that he is held accountable for all the duties necessary in the performance of their work.

There are, of course, limits to this as a general rule. These men have resided in the village for long periods

of time, and while the individuals who assume the head
cuttership change from time to time, the estate ownership is a powerful family of long standing, and highly
visible, duration. Therefore, the men owe their deepest
allegiances to the owners rather than the leaders of the
work gangs. Whenever really important problems arise,
such as a loan to buy a house, a grant for a house plot
or a job for a close relative, the men of course seek out
the owner and do not trouble with intermediaries.

2. *Pace Setting and Encouragement*

The head cutter's most important function is to exert
continual pressure to maintain the pace of the gang's
work. He can do this in several ways. As the man who
leads off, he establishes a standard pace the other cutters
must meet. When he finishes his first rows, he takes up
his next row behind the eleventh man. In this way he
not only can haul the gang along, but also, once the first
line has been cut, continually push against the gang from
the rear. He might also comment on the progress of the
other men while they are working. The men depend
upon him for this function, and without his effort, the
pace of the gang and the total output would fall off
significantly.

More than simply maintaining a steady pace is the
requirement that he keep the men on the job. If one of
the men gets "discouraged" and wishes to leave, it is the
head cutter's task to convince him to stay. A further
danger of "discouragement" is that a cutter who wishes
to leave will not go home alone. Because he wants to
hide in the total action of the group he attempts to convince all the other cutters to go home with him. At this
point the head cutter must step in, reason with the men,
and try to keep them in the field. If the head cutter cannot convince the men to stay, he always has the power,
within this system, to state that he will continue working
for the day. Therefore, any man who leaves the field will
be credited with only a fraction of the day's pay, while
the head cutter will receive the full day's pay, irrespective
of how little he cut the remainder of the day.

One of the best ways the head cutter can handle this
problem is to attempt to prevent it from ever occurring.

He tries to forestall the men from getting "discouraged" whenever problems begin to develop by maintaining a flow of banter among the men. Jokes have always served to lighten a burden. This process is known among the men as "encouragement"; they will work harder for the man they feel is "encouraging," and resent the one who is not. Another method is to share a small possession with the men. One morning, I gave a cigarette to a head cutter who was resting while the other men worked. He smoked about a quarter and then went over to the slowest man in the gang and gave it to him. Another time, while speaking to a different head cutter who was watching his men as he ate one of several bananas he had brought to the field, I noticed him suddenly reach into his bag, take out a banana and bring it over to one of his men. When he came back, I asked about it and he explained how necessary it is to "encourage" the men. He felt that if this kind of interest was not shown the men would get resentful and lose interest in their work.

A final method of "encouragement," or technique to prevent discouragement, which I observed in the field, was the occasional assistance the head cutter gives to a man who is either a slow worker, or else ill [5] on that particular day. If the man has been cutting very slowly, falling behind the pace of the gang and so disrupting the gang's rhythms, and is obviously in trouble, the head cutter will join him on his row and help cut out a portion of the cane. This restores the pattern of operation of the whole gang and ensures him that the man will be able to continue working for that day. If that man had gone home, his departure would have exerted a demoralizing effect on the rest of the men and might have led to a general slackening of the pace. The cutter's need for the presence of the total gang membership is so strong that it often forces the head cutter to seek the men out in the village and try to get them all to come up to the fields to work.

[5] These small debilitating illnesses, which greatly reduce the man's capacity for work, are quite frequent in Dieppe Bay. They are either due to a hangover following an evening's spree, or to a gastroenteritis disorder. These attacks are severe enough to weaken a man for several days.

There were two gangs on the estate whose contrasting work practices lay bare some of the underlying dynamics of the cane gang. One gang functioned smoothly and consistently turned in the highest tonnage of any gang on the estate. The other produced less tonnage and was continually the scene of quarrels. The first gang, by any prediction, should have had the worst performance of all three adult cutting gangs on this estate because they were the youngest and least experienced group. The second, on the other hand, was composed of strong young men with a great deal of experience.[6]

The difference between the performance of the two gangs lies in the degree to which each of their leaders fulfills the requirements of the head cutter's role. The second head cutter does not encourage the men when they do not feel like working. Whenever someone shows impatience with cutting, he tells them "Whoever wants to work, work. Whoever doesn't, go home!" He, himself, does not set a good example for the men because he does not like working when only a few men show up for work. In this way, he is like his own men, rather than one who possesses all those psychological qualities required of a head cutter. A number of times I noticed that his gang did not proceed with cutting because only three men came out. If he had begun on those days, I was told, it would have been quite likely that a number of the other men would have heard about it down in the village and would have come up.

The first head cutter has also made several innovations in the role of head cutter. Several years ago, he became disenchanted with his pattern of life, wasting his money on women and rum, and turned to a new Pentecostal church that had come into the village. Now he has given up cigarettes, rum and women, and devotes his entire energies to the activities of his church. Virtually every night some function is scheduled at the church, and he is always present playing his guitar. The emphasis placed by the church on Christian fellowship has carried over

[6] The third gang was composed of men in their thirties and forties and was known as the steady and mature group. However, because steadiness does not quite compensate for youth, it had the poorest record of the three.

to his manner of handling his gang. Although I overheard some of his men complain to the union representative that he will not allow joking on the grounds that it is obscene, the men feel that he is especially helpful and fair and so have been "encouraged" to produce more than was expected. For example, he will give men credit for a full day's work if they legitimately take sick during the day, while it is claimed that the other head cutter will not. He will also be more vigorous in stimulating the men to work. His men see the Christian ethic as having had direct influence on his attitudes toward the gang, as he will not always take the short row when the opportunity presents itself. Instead, he will occasionally gather the men together and supervise them as a unit until the short rows have been cut out.

3. Tolerance of Abuse

The cane cutters react to the frustrations of their job with a continual stream of complaints and abuse directed against the head cutter. Most of the cutters (14 of 17) felt that they would not want to assume the position because of the difficulties they, themselves, create for him. In answer to the question on the standard interview "Would you want to be a head cutter?" I received the following replies:

"No. Head cutter gets too much ill-treat. The men abuse him too much."
"Too much dispute. I rather work last."
"No. Too much bad name. Too much abusing."

The certainty that abuse will be his lot creates a demand for another set of attributes in the head cutter revolving around his response to the abuse. Some reaction to the frustration the men feel is inevitable, and it is even healthy from the point of view of the long-term maintenance of the gang that this outlet remain available to them. However, an appropriate method of dealing with this must exist.

The crucial aspect of the response is that the head cutter not over-react to the hostility shown him. There is a dynamic young man on the estate who had been a head cutter for a brief period the year before this study.

His difficulty came in that he was too hasty, got personally involved in every complaint and fought back. Returning aggression really made trouble, where none had existed before, and completely disrupted the working of the gang. Another case which came to my attention had occurred several years earlier. During a dispute with one of the gang, the head cutter, in his fury, slashed out at him with his machete and nearly severed the man's arm. As might be imagined, this made for some difficulty in the gang's continuing to work together, and that head cutter had to resign.

As a result, the role of head cutter vis-à-vis the men's aggression takes a clear-cut form. The head cutter must be tolerant of all complaints; he must listen to them quietly, or bear up under them stolidly. He must remain silent in the face of provocation—although there is a limit—and let the anger and tension in the men dissipate itself against him.

4. The Basis for Prestige in the Gang

The criteria by which cutters judge one another, and the means by which prestige is gained, are based on a person's position. In reply to the question on the Male Interview, "What makes the other men in the gang respect you?" the cutters presented the gang's structure as one in which there was a gulf between the position of head cutter and the homogeneous layer of men. Prestige, based on this differential, is given primarily to the head cutter. This is not an earned quality, but one attached to the position. When an individual occupies this position he rises above his fellows, in their eyes, and maintains this respect as long as he serves. Few of the cutters specify personal qualities as the sole grounds for respect. The men reply:

> "Only the head cutter gets respect. Only respect because you are over."
>
> "Respect the head cutter as he is set in authority over us."
>
> "Really supposed to respect the head cutter. He is the foreman."
>
> "The head cutter. He is responsible for the gang."

On the other hand, a few of the cutters did not

specify the role of head cutter. It is interesting to contrast their responses, for the difference between them reveals a great disparity in psychological meaning.

> "How you move and speak. Have a reason [reasoning] power."
> "How they act. Best of manners and respect. If he gives it to you, have respect for him."
> "A good working man. Good behavior."

These men evaluate their fellows in terms of personal qualities. Respect is earned by the capacity to work, general politeness, sobriety and intellectual ability. In other words, this basis of prestige is predicated upon the perception of the person and not the position.

One may classify the cutter's responses in three categories: those that fall into the above two groups, and a third category which combines a statement that the head cutter is the one to respect with mention of several personal qualities. To show the extent to which the cutters emphasize position as the basis of prestige, it is well to compare their responses with the fishermen's. This is done in Table 5-1.

TABLE 5-1

Bases of respect in the cane cutting gang and the fishing crew

	I Leader's Position	II Both Position and Personal Qualities	III Personal Qualities
Fishermen	2	0	13
Cane Cutters	5	5	3

I and II vs. III
$p < .005$
(Fisher test)

The difference is clear. Whereas the cutters focus on position as a basis of respect in ten of the thirteen cases, and just three men take only personal qualities into account, the reverse is found among the fishermen. They, in contrast, mention only personal qualities in thirteen of the fifteen cases, and but two base their respect on the position of the captain. This is a significant difference beyond the .005 level, with the Fisher exact probability test.

The reason for this difference, I believe, lies in the personalities of the men concerned and their ways of responding to their fellow workers. Cane cutters tend to fear other people and because of the shallowness of their evaluative experience respond to men on the basis of their position in the society. Fishermen, however, have the ability to perceive personal qualities in their fellow workers as well as the need to respond to them. Therefore, they can relate themselves to the whole group according to these principles. This difference will be discussed further in Chapter 7.

6

Comparative Materials
on the Cane Gang

We have seen, so far, a direct relationship between childhood experiences, adult personality and work group structure of the cane cutters of Dieppe Bay. The fishing crew, which will be examined in the next chapter, shows a great contrast in each phase of the personality-culture process. The comparison between these occupations will provide a means to isolate the significant factors and determine the sequence of events creating the final state of the economic units. Yet, it still remains to be shown that the sugar estate, as an institution, does not prescribe that reaping be carried out by the specific mechanism discovered on St. Kitts.

This chapter will present brief capsules of the way harvesting has been organized in other areas. This is important for three reasons. First, no matter how close the congruence between the cane gang and the fishing crew, it is still true that one is a unit within a larger stratified structure and the other a creation of relatively few individuals. It is necessary to demonstrate that the differences are not due to this fact. Second, the variation in form which is discovered in surveys of the literature on sugar plantations demonstrates that there is no essential institutional requirement that reaping be carried out through large, authoritarian cane gangs. This information will demonstrate the plasticity inherent in the form. Furthermore, these examples will show reaping to be performed in ways that can be related to the cane cutter's personality. Third, the significance of a new conceptualization rests in that conceptualization's ability to clarify phenomena other than those from which it was derived. The brief accounts to be reported here, and in Chapter 8 on the fishing crew, are evidence of the predictive power of this approach.

Before presenting this material, I would like to point out several qualifications. I have not gathered these reports as part of this study. They are, rather, isolated fragments of larger works directed to the particular purposes of their own authors. Therefore, equivalent information on all aspects of the reaping process was not available. Moreover, the tools which were used to gather these findings were not similar to those of this study. These data are not based on psychological tests, standard interviewing of selected samples, childhood questionnaires, nor the kind of detailed and limited ethnographic analysis of the estate structure attempted here. I have selected from these accounts that information which can throw some light on the broad problem at issue.[1]

One further word. In my search for comparative materials I have limited the examples to those of sugar cane estates in the circum-Caribbean area. My hope has been to narrow the focus to one broad historical and ecological zone.

I. AMITY: A TRINIDADIAN EAST INDIAN VILLAGE[2]

The cane reaping system in Amity is radically different from that which exists in Dieppe Bay. Cutters are assigned their area of the cane field by a driver, and thereafter are on their own. Each man works individually: he can start and end when he wishes. Since he has no one guiding his work, he can, and must, work at whatever pace he chooses. He is also free to cut as much or as little cane as he desires. Production is calculated by the task, which is the cutting of a section of the field containing approximately two tons of cane. After the man cuts his cane it is loaded into a cart by another man who is assigned to him alone. There is neither regulation nor support by any of the others working in the same field.

---

[1] It must be emphasized that the interpretation of these studies is solely my own responsibility.

[2] Klass, M. "Cultural Persistence in a Trinidad East Indian Community." Unpublished Ph.D. dissertation, Columbia University, 1959.

I believe there are several reasons why this system is so different. First, the East Indian in the Caribbean still retains much of his former cultural pattern. The differences between the East Indian and Negro in Trinidad have been analyzed by Morris Freilich (1960), who claims that the East Indian pattern of life, at present, is much more centered around the family than is the Negro. There is a much greater endurance of the marital relationship; a more intense system of requirements from each member; and a kinship unit based on ties of affection rather than on a less personal system of rights and obligations. This historically determined cultural difference provides a more stable family in which to grow and produces an individual less oriented to seek safety gratifications than those on St. Kitts.

Second, the East Indian came to Trinidad as an indentured servant, rather than as a slave. This held for him many benefits unavailable to the West Indian Negro, for he could always dream of going home and he had a similar culture to share with his fellows. Most important, he never went through all the experiences of the capture in Africa, the torments of the Middle Passage and a life or death relationship to a master on Trinidad.

Third, in order to induce the East Indians to remain near the estates and serve as a pool of labor, relatively soon after their arrival the estates either gave them plots of land or made Crown lands available. Today, these people live in a village they own and have small amounts of land to work nearby.

The possibility for private land ownership was an economic event with great psychological significance. Because he owns his own land the laborer is never totally dependent upon the estate. During the dull season (croptime is only 140 days) he has the income from the sale of provisions to maintain himself. The estate can never, as on St. Kitts, command him to move his house or threaten him with eviction if he does not obey orders. Nor may an estate manager humiliate him by coming into his yard and plucking the fruit from his trees, as I have witnessed on St. Kitts. Having land of their own gives the family roots and exerts a cohesive force counter to all those pulling it apart. For the resident these factors provide an orientation of stability and control over their own lives which is greatly lacking on St. Kitts. From a psychological point of view, this assures the individual person of a more constant and varied supply of food, thereby satisfying his physiological needs. The greater stability in the family provides for increased gratification of safety and love needs and yields individuals who can function well on the self-esteem level. Out of this milieu can arise men who have little need to create safety gratifying mechanisms like the cane gang.

II. CHALKY MOUNT: A NEGRO VILLAGE IN THE HIGHLANDS OF BARBADOS[3]

Amity provides the first example of a different method of cutting sugar cane. The system in Chalky Mount yields similar evidence and is of more direct value, as the population is Negro with an English colonial heritage, rather than East Indian. Therefore, the racial and historical factors are more comparable to the cutters of Dieppe Bay. In this village cane is cut in two ways. The first procedure involves two or three men, of approximately equal ability, who are friends and choose to work together. This is a purely voluntary association and lasts as long as the members work in harmony. The estate managers are not concerned with its composition, and all the internal decisions, such as the amount of cane to be cut daily and the pace of cutting, are left up to the men to determine. In the second method, which is dominant in Chalky Mount, the men cut cane individually in a system directly analogous to the one in Amity. Again, there is no provision for a leader comparable to the head cutter of St. Kitts. The manager limits himself to choosing the field to be cut and the area in the field assigned to each man. Thereafter, the cutter carries out his task, for which he is rewarded individually, in the manner he sees fit.

Ownership of land among the cutters of Chalky Mount is also similar to the pattern in Amity. The

[3] Handler, J. "Land Exploitative Activities and Economic Patterns in a Barbados Village." Unpublished Ph.D. dissertation, Brandeis University, 1965.

laborers own both their house plots and small parcels of land near the village on which they grow ground provisions and sugar cane. Of further importance is the fact that virtually all residents of Chalky Mount are native born to the village. It should be remembered that over half of the cane cutters on St. Kitts were immigrants from other islands. These two factors, ownership of land and birth in village contribute, I believe, to a personality not as dominated by needs for safety as on St. Kitts, and result in an economic arrangement based to a large part on interpersonal ties and individual initiative.

There is also an important social development which contrasts with the shallowness of inter-personal communication of the cane-cutting subculture on St. Kitts. The predominant characteristics of the Kittitian cane cutters were isolation and mistrust, and as a group they showed little cooperation and solidarity. In Chalky Mount, on the other hand, the cutters had an institution known as "keeping meeting." This is a system in which a number of cutters decide to contribute a fixed amount of money (up to $5) to a pool. Each week one man's name is drawn, and he receives the sum until every person in the pool has had his chance at the big money. As a group endeavor, this demands lack of suspicion, willingness to participate with other people, a commitment to a substantial outlay of money for a long period of time and a deep enough understanding of the group to compel a person to continue paying even after he has won his turn. In light of the lack of solidarity on St. Kitts, this is a remarkable achievement.

III. BRITISH GUIANA: NEGRO AND EAST INDIAN
CANE CUTTERS

(a) Report of a Commission of Inquiry into the Sugar Industry of British Guiana (1949).
(b) Jayawardena (1963).

Jayawardena states that cane cutting on the estates he studied in British Guiana is performed individually. Each man in the field works at his own pace and is responsible for loading whatever he cuts into a small boat in the canal near the field. (The cane fields in British Guiana are surrounded by canals.) The cane that the cutter places into the boat is sent to the factory where it is weighed, and he is credited with that amount. On the estates visited by the Commission, where the cutters were predominantly Negro, the work was done by two men laboring as a unit, as in Chalky Mount. They cut and loaded the punt and shared the results of their labor. Neither of the two men acted as driver to the other.[4]

Of even greater interest is the extraordinary emphasis on solidarity found by Jayawardena among the East Indian laborers on the sugar estate, which they term "Mati." It is conceived of as a feeling of commonality that can be "broken" by people performing aggressive or individualistic acts against their fellows or by breaking ranks in disputes with management. This is indeed a far cry from St. Kitts.

Jayawardena accounts for "Mati" on the grounds that it is essential for the workers to maintain a common front and act with loyalty to their group in their dealings with the estate management. One would expect "Mati" to be equally useful to the cane cutters of St. Kitts and, therefore, a universal feature of the cane cutting gang, or work groups of this type, in general. Yet, not only is there no solidarity of this kind to be found in Dieppe Bay gangs, but all too frequently the cutters try to raise themselves by hurting their friends.

Among the East Indian workers, the central topic of disputes involves attempts to belittle or attack a man's dignity and prestige. This they call "eye-pass," as in the expression "You take you eye and pass me" (p. 72).[5] Jayawardena lists several synonyms for this offense, such as "take advantage 'pon, become biggity, play big', play power-man" (p. 72). Through "eye-pass" the offender

[4] Further examples of men cutting sugar cane individually may be found in the studies of Mintz (1956) and Hay (1961), reporting the practices of estates on Puerto Rico and Guadeloupe, respectively.

[5] C. Jayawardena, *Conflict and Solidarity in a Guianese Plantation.*

deviates from the equalitarian code by asserting claims to a superior status. The group studied was hypersensitive to this kind of behavior, retaliating verbally and physically whenever it appeared. To anticipate the discussion in Chapter 7 in which a similar phenomenon was found among the fishermen of Dieppe Bay, concern over "eye-pass" may be interpreted as an excessive demand for self-esteem gratifications by a group who, though having reached this level, find few other chances to satisfy their now dominant need.

In the areas studied by the Commission the Negro workers held privately owned lands. After emancipation the Negro slaves moved off the estates and took over possession of nearby vacant land, on which they had their villages and land to grow provisions and rice. This situation led to psychological advantages similar to those discussed earlier.

The Commission report mentions a further factor, non-existent on St. Kitts, which we might expect would produce a healthier personality. They state that historically there has always been a system of crèche houses in operation to care for the children while their mothers worked. One great problem I became aware of on St. Kitts is that when the father deserts the mother, often she has no one to look after her children while she is in the fields, and frequently is forced to turn the children over to other people. Because of this, the desertion or emigration of the father often means loss of the mother as well. To the extent that the system of crèche houses has been an actuality in British Guiana, it has served to lessen the insecurity in the life of the growing child.

The East Indians studied by Jayawardena were brought to British Guiana after the Negro working force had moved off the plantation and took possession of the un-used land. As a result they have remained on estate property and, in contrast to the Negro workers, do not hold land of their own. The significant factor leading to a population functioning on higher levels of personality, in their case, is the continuation of their former cultural patterns which maintain the stability of the family. In this way, they demonstrate to us that a work group structure based on non-security oriented principles is not a function of subsidiary peasant activities. Rather, it establishes that a variety of factors are influential in gratifying lower needs and that the key to understanding economic units of this kind lies in an examination of the predominant needs the workers are attempting to gratify.

7

The Fishing Crew

Although St. Kitts is entirely surrounded by water, the scarcity of beaches and rockiness of the coast bars fishing from all but a few villages. Only six of the approximately thirty villages and towns engage in fishing to any extent. Dieppe Bay is, then, an atypical village for St. Kitts and the only substantial fishing community on the Atlantic side of the island. This is due to the presence of a barrier reef which provides the village with a small safe harbor for launching boats, a calm fishing area during the hazardous winter months and protection against the churning seas of the hurricane season. In this way, the physical characteristics of Dieppe Bay hold out to its residents the potential for an alternative occupation not directly dependent upon the estates.

I. RECRUITMENT, TRAINING, AND FORMATION OF THE CREW

1. *The Psychological Demands and Gratifications of Fishing*

Fishing, however, is not simply an alternative occupation to cane cutting, for in many fundamental respects it has different goals, uses different means and requires radically different personnel. The first indication of the divergence is evident when we examine the ages at which the fishermen began work. Whereas cane cutters entered in late adolescence, fishermen began work (as fishermen) around the age of thirty. The median age for entering fishing was 29.5 years.

This initial variation is due, I believe, to those psychological demands made by fishing which cannot be met by the young boy. Fishing compels the worker to appear for work each day, or else the crew cannot func-

114

tion. Unlike the cane cutter, he must guarantee his presence or else be fired. For the young man, who is at that time more interested in the discovery of himself as an adult, and is not yet forced to provide for a large household, this is too great a commitment. Moreover, fishing makes demands for self-direction, responsibility and thinking impossible for one not committed to this field. Finally, pot fishing requires that money be put aside from a weekly salary until a substantial sum is saved. When an individual's goals demand more immediate gratifications, this becomes an obstacle which is virtually impossible to overcome.

For these reasons, one pattern of gradually breaking into fishing has been for a man to work on the estate during croptime and fish when the reaping of the cane has been completed. This, fortunately, coincides with the arrival of the gar fishing season. Garfish travel in large schools and are sought by different means than pot fish. Usually four men work together in a crew under the direction of a captain, who may own the large net used in the catch. This is an excellent transition from estate work to fishing. Although requiring constant attendance, gar fishing does not obligate the man to invest money nor demand that he take over direction of self, which are among the duties of the captain. In this way the gar fishing crew is somewhat similar to the cane gang and so is attractive to these men—especially at a time of year when work on the estate is at a minimum and wages are extremely low. Many of the fishermen in my sample began work on the bay during the gar season, after working in the cane most of the year. When the men became older they left the estate and entered fishing full time.

In order to comprehend crew structure it is crucial to understand the forces which bring men into this occupation. The men explained their motivations in answer to the questions, "Why did you choose fishing?" and "Do you prefer cane cutting or fishing?" on the Male Interview.

"More independent. I go when I wants to go. No compulsion. No one can make me go. I likes that."
"To ease me away from the hard work what I ain't getting

no money from. Too much work and no money. When you get something, it is a good amount."

"Like the sea water. I couldn't get on with Manager of estate. Felt [I was] getting old [and] tired of managers. No manager could revenge you."

". . . I don't appreciate managers. Too rude."

"The whole family runs to heredity."

"[I] like the sea. Planet was connected with the sea."

"I love it."

"No other job as good as that . . . Can make more money in one day than the fellow in the field makes a week."

"Don't like cutting cane. Too much advantage they take."

"No man can stop your money."

"I can choose to come in if rain falls or sun too hot. But in cane must stay there."

"If you are tired you can come home. You have no driver."

These statements revolve around four main issues. First, they stress the fact that as fishermen they are independent, self-motivated and in control over their own actions. Second, the pay is good. But even more important, when money comes in it is in large amounts and enables them to make substantial purchases if they wish (a boat, a house, a party). Third, they are not exploited physically, psychologically, or financially. Last, the pursuit of the fishing trade holds out intrinsic rewards and makes them feel attuned to the job—"planet was connected with the sea," "I love it."

Two points must be stressed. From the tone of their responses we may conclude that the fishermen enjoy their

TABLE 7-1 [1]

Preference of occupation for cane cutters and fishermen

	Expressed Preference	
	Fishing	Cane Cutting
Fishermen	17	0
Cane Cutters	10	10

[1] The validity of the general hypothesis depends upon a comparison of the structure of the two groups. This chapter presents statistical data on the various issues, some of which has been offered in Chapter 5 for cutters alone.

TABLE 7-2

Previous occupation of fishermen and cutters

Occupation of Fishermen	Number of Men	Occupation of Cane Cutters	Number of Men
1. Cutter	3	1. Hander	2
2. Cutter, then Packer	2	2. Packer	2
3. Packer	4	3. Day Work	2
4. Day Work	1	4. Sailor	1
5. Laborer	1	5. Laborer	1
6. Carpenter	2	6. Sharecropper	1
7. Baker	1	7. Always cutter	12
8. Inspector of Schools	1		
9. Always Fishermen	4		

work. This is especially true when their answers are compared with those of the cane cutters. To the question of desirability of the trade the fishermen were unanimous in choosing fishing to cutting cane, while half of the cane cutters recognized fishing as the preferable trade. See Table 7-1.

A second point of comparison is the number of jobs held previous to the present one. Whereas most of the cane cutters started and continued in cane, the majority of fishermen held other kinds of jobs before they began fishing. These data are presented in Table 7-2, and summarized in Table 7-3.

From these materials we may conclude that fishermen

TABLE 7-3

Previous occupation of fishermen and cutters

	No Previous Occupation	Previous Occupation
Fishermen	4	15
Cutters	12	9

$$X^2 = 4.01$$
$$p < .025$$

change their jobs because they are looking for one that permits them to exert control over their activities and escape the exploitation of the estate. Also, they seem to have searched for work that can offer some intrinsic pleasure. As a comparison of group processes, the lack of previous occupation illustrates the need for safety in the cutters; they have found their niche and stay in it. Fishermen, in contrast, do not need the security offered by the gang, resent the estate bureaucracy and the confining nature of a large gang and search for a better means of making a living.

This process was demonstrated quite clearly on the projective tests. While the cane cutters were mostly concerned with safety needs, the fishermen scored high on the need for self-esteem. Furthermore, to the extent that it was possible to score for self-actualization needs, the fishermen were seen to be involved in activities that gave some degree of intrinsic pleasure, while the cane cutters preferred, in their own words, "to stay neutral."

To support this argument it is necessary to examine the occupation of their fathers, which is often an important determinant of occupational choice. Fishing is a trade requiring a certain degree of knowledge, and it might be expected that the fishermen learned their skills from fathers who were themselves fishermen. If this were true then the basis of recruitment in fishing would not be

TABLE 7-4

Occupation of father

Occupation of Fisherman's Father	Number of Fathers	Occupation of Cane Cutter's Father	Number of Fathers
1. Cut cane	1	1. Cut cane	3
2. Other estate work	2	2. Other estate work	1
3. Cut cane and fished	2	3. Cut cane and fished	1
4. Fished	3	4. Fished	3
5. Had his own land	3	5. Had his own land	2
6. Laborer on other people's land	1	6. Factory	1
7. Carpenter	2	7. Carpenter	2
8. Estate Manager	1	8. Tailor	1
9. Unknown	4	9. Unknown	7

psychological needs, but rather a form of an occupational caste system. Table 7-4 presents the fathers' occupations. It is most relevant to notice the frequency of fathers, in both groups, whose livelihood was fishing. A number of the men did not know their fathers so parental occupation could not have been a significant influence on them. Of the men who did know their fathers, if we count those fathers who both fished and cut cane as both fishermen and cane cutters, then the frequency of fathers who were fishermen is about the same. The cane cutters had 4 of 14 fathers, and the fishermen had 5 of 15 fathers, who were engaged in the fishing trade. Therefore, as no trend toward a similar parental occupation characterizes either group, we may conclude that parental occupation is not an important factor in determining choice of occupation.

2. *The Kinship Basis of the Fishing Crew*

The organization these men create differs in a further regard from that of the cane gang. One of the important aspects of the crew appears to be kinship ties, as most of the fishermen have close relatives in fishing. Although they do not necessarily fish with each other, and several do not live in the village, the most active fishermen in Dieppe Bay at present are a group of brothers and cousins.[2] This is much less true for cane cutters, as may be seen in Table 7-5. The significant question is why so many fishermen are related, as it is not enough to merely describe the kinship aspects of fishing. A causal analysis must seek to determine the reasons for this degree of kinship relationships.

Two principles of formation seem to be involved in determining the kinship basis of the fishing crew. First, virtually all the fishermen are native born Kittitians; either born in Dieppe Bay or the neighboring villages. Recall that 52% of the cane cutters were born outside of St. Kitts. See Table 7-6. A second factor which throws light on this problem was discovered when I correlated the

[2] It is interesting that the only aspect of crew structure in which kinship ties operate is in the preference given in the recruitment of members. In all other operations of the crew no distinction is made.

Table 7-5

Relatives in the same occupation

	Relatives in Occupation	No Relatives In Occupation
Fishermen	14	5
Cutters	8	12

$$x^2 = 3.23$$
$$p < .05$$

answer the fishermen gave to the question, "Who taught you to fish?" with their place of origin. I found that when a man claims to have been taught by a specific individual he has usually grown up in the village with

Table 7-6

Birthplace and occupation

	Born on St. Kitts	Born Outside St. Kitts
Fishermen	15	3
Cutters	10	11

$$x^2 = 3.99$$
$$p < .025$$

him. These individual teachers are not necessarily kinsmen. In fact, it is rare for a fisherman whose father was also a fisherman to have been taught by him. Usually, he was taught by a non-related person. When he has not grown up in the village in which he will learn the fishing trade, he claims that "no one in particular" was his teacher. Instead, these men state that they learned their skills just by "hanging around with the men." This is presented in Table 7-7.

I believe that recruitment into the crew along kinship ties is based on the way Kittitians handle aggression. The British have fostered, throughout the colonial period, a highly repressive judicial system. Police are extremely alert

TABLE 7-7

Trainer of fishermen and village of birth

	Trainer of Fishermen	
	Specific Person	No Specific Person
Born in the village where trained	9	1
Not born in the village where trained	2	6
		$p < .005$ (Fisher test)

to any overt act of violence and, generally, having achieved this goal, institute a policy of suppressing verbal acts of aggression. These cases of "abusive language" now dominate the rural courtroom. This has gone to such an extreme that during my stay one man was arrested one night for cursing while he was walking down the street dead-drunk. The complaint read that he was "abusing himself"! Historically, this system was designed to suppress not only rebellion, but all conflict among the population in general. The purpose, we may speculate, was to let nothing lessen the laborer's ability as a worker. Today, individual people have great power over each other, because they can summon the strength of the court in their quarrels with their neighbors. The court hands down summary fines and imprisonments usually favoring the plaintiff.

The ones who feel the brunt of this system are those who are different in some way. There seems to be a general practice to focus on any peculiarity of an individual and use him as the scapegoat for all the frustrations of life. In Dieppe Bay, for example, there was great horror expressed at the person of a man who had once had leprosy and lost several digits of his fingers. Even though completely cured, he was avoided and mocked. Another case of the same phenomenon took place with a woman who, though merely suffering from acne, was tormented by the villagers who accused her of having leprosy. But the largest category of victims are those called "strangers." It is possible to move into the village from a neighboring one, forty years earlier, marry a Dieppe Bay girl, have many Dieppe Bay children and still be looked on as an "outsider." For those newly arrived the process of out-group aggression is very strong. In the village they feel themselves always in a state of marginality and are therefore much less likely to take recourse to the judiciary. This is because they must live in the village and feel that they are not likely to be supported by the village population if they do. These factors militate against a state of equal degree of the release of aggression.

Perhaps more basic in the process of selecting outsiders to be the objects of aggression is the fact that native-born residents of the village have intimate knowledge of the people with whom they grow up, and much less understanding of those who are newly arrived. As a general psychological rule, it seems true that there is a direct relation between degree of frustration and anger or hatred. One means they have to handle these feelings is through projection. Also, the less you know about a person the more dangerous he appears, and the more he is to be shunned. This is what happens to the new migrants, who draw to themselves a great deal of the general tensions of the village. However, those with whom the villagers have spent their lives are known, are not as likely to be suspect, and, therefore, do not so easily serve as the objects of projected aggression.

These two principles, mistrust of outsiders as a form of projected aggression, and the lack of support strangers receive by the total village population, combined to place those people who were not born in the village in an extremely marginal position. It is possible to imagine this process as a dimension reaching from the very well-known (a brother) to the absolute stranger (an immigrant from Nevis) and the degree of familiarity determining one's relationship to the village.

This attitude toward strangers is central to the formation of the fishing crew. In order to become a fisherman, it is necessary to learn the skills of the trade, understand the rocks and waters, and work in close relationship to other men. Because the fishermen are also participants in this process of out-group aggression, it is difficult to get one to teach a stranger the trade. If a stranger cannot find a mentor then it is quite difficult to train himself. Even with men from Dieppe Bay there is the continual complaint that those who do possess the knowledge are reluctant, "grudge" as they say, to teach it to others. This is why those men who were not born in Dieppe Bay state that "no specific person" taught them to fish, and have had to find the skills and contacts by themselves. This process explains why most of the men on the bay are from Dieppe Bay and neighboring villages and why fishing is often a family affair; for they are much less likely to "grudge" family than strangers.

II. STRUCTURE OF THE CREW

A. *The Gar Boat Crew*

1. *The Ecological Demand on the Work Group.* Gar fishing is different, in many respects, from cane cutting and pot fishing. The fish travel in large schools and are caught by a long net which requires intimate, synchronized and immediate cooperation among the members of the crew. Typically, the boat travels out to selected waters near the village where the men throw pieces of dry cane trash on the water to attract the fish. The gar fish enjoy playing with the floating trash and thus are drawn together. The captain is usually at the tiller while three men row the boat. When the fish are spotted and begin sporting with the trash, the captain throws out the first part of the net and the boat makes a sweep around the school of fish. As the men quickly bend to their oars, the captain lets out the net and throws rocks into the area not yet reached in order to prevent an escape and to drive the fish back into the net. When the fish are encircled one man, who stands up in the prow of the boat, picks up the cork line while the captain begins pulling in the heavily weighted net at the other end. During this time one of the crewmen beats the water with his oar in order to frighten the fish into the seine, where their slender extended bodies and long beaks become entangled in the netting. This takes place with a

great burst of energy and must be extremely well co-ordinated in order to be successful.

Ideally, the gar crew is composed of five men: a captain, a second—who can act as the captain if necessary —two men and a spare. The spare man is the one who rests on a particular day, and the rest period is alternated among all the men, excluding the captain. When a man is resting he is still considered as a member of the crew and shares equally in the catch.

One can see the contrast with the cane gang. The most obvious is the ecological necessity that the crew be an integrated group of men who function well as a unit. There can be no mistrust or slackening of one's particular task or else the effort as a whole will fail.

2. *Relation of Captain to Crew.* A second difference with the cane gang lies in the relationship of the captain to his men.[3] Whereas in the cane there was a great gulf between the head cutter and men, with the head cutter taking a great deal of advantage of the men, this is not found in gar fishing. In this work group there are much closer ties and a determination that the captain not set himself too far above the men or push them around. If he attempts to do this the men refuse to work with him any longer and leave. There have been many cases in which a gar crew quit rather than work with a "bad" captain. At present there are two people who own nets and boats, but none of the men would go out under them because, as one fisherman explained to me, "he too bolden." Even more, in the gar boat there is the understanding that the men have a right to decide where to go, or may veto a command they do not like. The captain must consult with his men or they will put their oars down and refuse to continue working. In the cane the problem was that the men would not attack the head cutter and force a change. When the men have the psychological capacity to do this, and have the potential power within the institution, then a much more integrated and democratic unit can develop.

The psychological capacities underlying the structure

[3] This relationship is not a function of ecological requirements on crew structure. See p. 156 for examples of alternative methods.

of the gar fishing crew are clearly evident. Of the fifteen men who were engaged in gar fishing during the season I observed, eleven can be scored as having had a low degree of loss in childhood. Two have had a high, although not unambiguously high, degree of loss, and for the final two I have no data. Six of the men are full-time fishermen and the rest estate laborers. Many of these estate workers are quite young and, it is safe to conclude, some will enter fishing as a full-time occupation in the next few years. Indeed, some are quite restive, at present, and are beginning to save money for fish pots. That this kind of work demands certain psychological qualities is shown by the fact that although the boats and nets are available, the market unfilled, the supply in the sea plentiful and the estate paying on the average only six dollars a week for two days work, few of the under-employed estate workers enter a gar fishing crew.

As the system functions, presently, the boat and net are usually owned by the captain, who hires the men and organizes them into a crew. He assumes most of the responsibility and provides most of the leadership. In this way his position is similar in function to the head cutter. Occasionally, a non-fisherman will purchase the boat and net as an investment and hire one man to fill the duties of the captain. Under this system, briefly, the owner of the equipment takes a 45% share of the catch, and the men divide the remaining 55%.

Gar fishing is a typical small-time capitalistic venture in which one man invests his money and assumes all the risks and responsibilities in return for his substantial share. We must realize that this implies the reduction of the crewmen's income by that much, which can amount to a great deal of money. From the records I kept of the day-by-day catch of the gar fishing boats, the share going to the owner can amount to $1,400, which is enough to pay for a new nylon net in one year. Thereafter, all is profit. One of the owner-captains, who had just bought a new nylon net, expected to be able to retire on the income from his nets when he got old.

"The Syndicate." Four of the fishermen, several years ago, tried to compensate for the large share of the catch

which goes to the owner of the net by instituting a change in the system. Their simple correction was to join together, pool their resources and purchase the equipment in a partnership. This venture they called a "syndicate," and it was a way of increasing their income by establishing a radically different form of ownership. Each of these men contributed $90 for the purchase of the net. For this small sum each man could be an owner, and receive a fourth of the net share which previously would have gone to the owner. Calculating the return for that year, approximately, on the basis of an average man's share of $20 per week, the net share was worth a total of $60 per week. Therefore, each man's share of the net was an extra $15 per week, which yielded a return to each man of approximately $300 extra over a five month gar season. Although this figure should be somewhat reduced, because of money taken out for repairs to the net, it is still a substantial return on an investment.

Yet the syndicate soon collapsed. The reasons for its breakup are extremely interesting and bring out some of the fundamental psychological prerequisites for this kind of economic structure. The first man who sold out claimed that the other men refused to give him his share when he had been sick for a week and was unable to fish. Another man put the blame on the "others" who would not come down to the beach to spread the net out on the sand to dry after a rain. He also complained that "they" did not show up when the net needed mending. So much contention arose over who had the responsibility and real or imagined wrongs that they decided to discontinue the syndicate.

Its demise, however, is very useful for our understanding the nature of fishing.[4] While the fishermen have the capacity to work closely with others to a degree unimaginable for the cane cutters, they have not yet reached the stage where they can share possessions and assume

[4] The rise and fall of the "syndicate" provides an example of an ongoing naturalistic experiment similar to the development of the "broken gang" on the estate. Both events allow the witnessing of those processes through which sociocultural institutions are formed (or not formed).

joint responsibility. They still have both the need to hurt and the mistrust of others which precludes a true and lasting form of cooperation. I asked the fishermen on the Male Interview "Would you ever get together with another fisherman to buy a boat or a net?" Only five of sixteen said they are for a partnership—even in theory. And these five included several who would only enter one with a son. As one man answered with the clear and pithy phrase: "A partnership is a leaky ship."

B. *The Pot Fish Crew*

The predominant form of fishing in Dieppe Bay is the pot fish crew which is organized in a number of different ways. It is profitable to discuss each in turn, so that we may see the general underlying principles.

1) In one system, the fisherman who owns a boat arranges to go out with two other fishermen. These men serve as his crew and do most of the labor; they row the boat out to the fishing grounds and pull the traps up from the bottom while he sits at the tiller. Typically, he has a large number of pots, perhaps twenty to thirty, and his men have just a few—anywhere from three to eight. Their system of sharing the catch is the same as in all the other variations of crew organization to be discussed. Each man keeps half of whatever is found in his own pot and places the other half in a pool to be shared equally by everyone, with a further share for the use of the boat. A three-man crew, then, will share the pool four ways. In this system, the captain who owns most of the pots and the boat receives virtually all the fish which are caught. He is able to keep 75% of his own catch (his half share plus the boat share plus his share of the catch) which is, generally, most of what has been caught. The crewmen, therefore, are dependent on the captain's catch.

2) In a second arrangement, a variation of the first, three men fish together; one buys many pots and serves as captain, the others have few and do the laboring. The difference between this type and the last lies in the ownership of the boat. Here the boat is rented from one of the other fishermen on a more or less permanent basis, which may continue for months to years. In return for

the use of the boat the men pay to the owner a portion of the catch known as the "boat share." Typically, with a three-man crew this is 12.5% of the total catch.

The question which concerns us is why the captain, who is a full-time fisherman with a long-standing commitment to fishing, rents rather than owns the boat. By this arrangement he stands to lose a continual 12.5% of his catch, which over the years can amount to a substantial sum of money. For example, assuming the captain's income averages thirty dollars a week over the year, this is a total loss to him of about $168 per year. If the cost of a boat in Dieppe Bay was high, then his renting of it would make a good deal of sense. However, from the purchase price of several boats in the village, which I was able to obtain, this is not the case. A small used boat was bought in 1962 for the sum of thirty dollars, and a medium size boat was purchased for ninety dollars. Finally, the cost of a large sail boat is around two hundred dollars. From these figures we can determine that a boat would be paid for by just what the captain pays out in rent in anywhere from a few months to a year. Loans from village storekeepers are also available at no interest. I have determined that several fishermen at various times have borrowed money from one man with whom they are on very good terms. Also, one fisherman, unique in the village in his ambition to possess good boats and nets, was able to borrow a considerable sum from the estate owner and was charged no interest. Finally, I am confident, and know it to have been the case in the "syndicate" previously discussed, that individuals who own equipment and wish to sell will accept payments over time.

The basis of this rental system, therefore, does not rest on the lack of available capital. Indeed, this arrangement makes little sense if approached from a strictly economic point of view. We should, rather, view this as an individual reaction to the dangers which threaten equipment in general. There have been several cases of boats having been caught in a storm and swamped. Moreover, ownership of equipment demands continual concern for its preservation. Boats must be caulked and painted, repairs are often required and an owner must be perpetually alert to any danger which might befall it. For example, if a storm blows up at night the owner must awaken some of his friends to help pull the boat to safety on higher land.

Furthermore, in the village population there are some envious of those who possess tangible property. This is called "grudging," and I have heard of many instances in which property was maliciously damaged. Parts of boats have been stolen and sometimes the sides have been staved in. Nets, which are left folded in piles on the beaches, are often cut or have pieces of the rope taken. Several times people have cut a rope, willfully, so that when the net is being hauled into the boat there would be no support of the strain, and the net would rip apart. There was even one instance when someone threw acid on a net and when it was put in the ocean it disintegrated.

One important captain pointed to this malicious damage when he was explaining why he rented a boat and did not want to own any equipment. He explained it by shaking his head and stating simply, "Black people are too bad." This refusal to invest in equipment demonstrates a fear, on the part of several individuals, to take a chance with, what is for Dieppe Bay fishing, part of the normal hazards of the trade. Not all the men, of course, are affected equally by these events. Some invest relatively heavily and look upon the destruction of their property as just one more burden to be overcome. The others, while they can cope with the uncertainties of their income and the inevitable loss of their traps to the sea, feel that this is a degree of loss that cannot be borne. Therefore, they flee the responsibilities of ownership and gladly pay the price of a rental system.

3) A third type of crew is composed of an experienced full-time fisherman, who owns the boat and many pots, and two inexperienced boys who own none. The composition of this crew does not function on a consistent basis. Whenever the captain desires to go out to his pots he calls two young men, from a pool of perhaps a dozen in the village, to go out with him for that day alone. These men are each paid for their labor by a one-eighth share of that day's catch. He may go out once, twice, or three times a week and the crewmen may vary every time. I

will present the specific drawbacks to this structure below, p. 131.

A variation of this arrangement is when the captain uses a rented boat. This is the worst of all the crew structures. It combines all the bad features of the above with the extra one of renting a boat.

The type 3 crew is generally used in one of three cases. It may occur when a fisherman has had a fight with his steady crew (type 1, 2 or 4) and decides he prefers to fish alone. (Relying on a stream of inexperienced boys is considered fishing alone.) Or this system might be used as a part-time measure by a man who is a committed member of a gar crew during the gar season. Last, there are several fishermen in the village who are cantankerous individuals and do not wish to be tied down to a stable involvement with their peers. Their desire to do just as they wish and go where and when they will makes them shun an organized crew. Possibly, as well, they may be disliked by the other fishermen who do not care for their company.

4) The most common crew structure in Dieppe Bay, and the one which functions best, involves two,[5] or occasionally three, full-time fishermen. They are experienced in their trade and own fifteen to thirty pots apiece. The man who owns the boat acts as the captain and the others as the crew. However, although they fill two different positions within the crew there is not the great gulf between statuses seen in the cane gang, or even the distance existing in the other crews. The captain retains the authority, which accrues both from his position and ownership of the boat, yet the crew is not predicated on an authoritarian base. These are usually crews composed of peers, men who have known each other for a long time, trust each other well and function generally on a basis of equality in all decision-making processes.

The benefits which this arrangement yields are many:

a. All the men in the crew have a substantial number of pots. Whereas crews 1, 2, and 3 might have anywhere from fifteen to, at the most, thirty pots, crew 4 may total fifty; which means that crew 4 has that much more

---

[5] When there are two experienced men they may take along one other person with just a few pots. The benefits that accrue to this type still hold true.

chance to catch fish. Greater numbers of traps enhance
the crew's potential not only because more pots bring in
more fish, but as they may be placed on different fishing
grounds, they reduce the risks when fish swim away. This
stabilizes the crew's yield, for if pots are set in only a
few areas the crew does not know what grounds the fish
are visiting when pots stop yielding. Having several pots
in different areas enables the crew to know where to go.

b. Occasionally a man falls ill. When there are several
experienced men, each can substitute for the other. These
men know where the pots of all crewmen are located
and can find that spot and pull the pots. Because the spot
where a pot is set is noted by triangulation with striking
objects on land, for example, trees, churches, houses, it
takes a good deal of experience with the "marks" before
someone can service another man's pots. Furthermore,
when the other crewmen in the boat are well trained,
they are competent to move that pot to another area
which they suspect might be productive if the pot has
failed to yield.

c. Crews 1, 2, and 3, include several inexperienced
men, who do not necessarily possess all the required skills.
They make errors which occasionally result in one of the
captain's pots being carried away. Also in those crews the
fund of knowledge and intuition is limited to one man.
All of these dangers are overcome in the present arrangement.

d. Frequently a boat has to go out to sea quickly. One
instance occurs when the sea suddenly begins a surging
the fishermen suspect will last several days. They may
wish to move their pots to safer waters, or else may know
that the rope on a given fish pot is somewhat frayed and
must be changed before the sea snaps the rope and takes
the pot away. Problems such as these arise often and
require immediate action by a trained crew. A captain
who has been fishing with inexperienced men cannot
count on getting the men to go out with him at just that
specific moment. Renting a boat is worse as the owner
might be using it at just that time, which keeps the
renter from going out altogether. These dangers are, of
course, obviated when the captain owns the boat himself and has a stable agreement with other fishermen.

The main characteristic of crew 4 is the degree to which it is a non-stratified, integrated structure. In contrast with the cutting gang and crews 1, 2, and 3, the captain of this crew functions as a first among equals. Although his authority is quickly challenged when the men feel that he has gotten out of line, he is generally respected for his abilities and the concern he usually takes for his men. There is not the constant abuse and complaining against the leader in this crew which one finds in the cane gang.

The reponses the men gave on the Sentence Completion Test to the stems "a head cutter," or "a captain," respectively, demonstrate the different relationship the leader has in each work group. The cutters see their head in two ways; either out to take advantage of them or else responsible for the work. They respond with such phrases as: "takes advantage of you," or "to see work goes all right." The modal response of the fishermen, though, is a category in which there are no comparable cane-cutter completions. This is the category of helpfulness and solidarity. Fishermen, in this group, respond with such comments as "is good and trusty"; "He looks to see I make a penny"; "tries to help each and every one of us." See Table 7-8.

This pattern of integration is evident in the way the crew usually handles disputes. To the question on the Interview "What happens if the crewmen don't agree with the captain?", the answers typically revolve around unity, consultation, and permitting everyone a chance to speak. Some of the answers were: "Boat will consider matters and come right under one heading"; "Captain will try what they say"; "first does what the captain wants to do, and then what the crew wants." Although the captain is given the respect and preference due to his generally greater knowledge and the fact that he owns the boat, there is little authoritarianism in crew functioning in Dieppe Bay.

The basis for the integrated, cooperative behavior among all the members of the crew, which is evident, for example, in their helping each other build fish pots, sharing fish when a crew member has no luck and the solidarity with which they stand up to their captain, lies

TABLE 7-8 [6]

Responses to the sentence completion stem:
"A head cutter" or "a captain"

| | "A Head Cutter" or "A Captain" | | |
	I Complaints, Takes Advantage	II Responsible for Job	III Helpful and Nurturant	IV Neutral
Fishermen	0	5	8	2
Cane Cutters	5	9	0	3

in the way the men feel about themselves and about their fellows. Cane cutters, we have seen, suspect the men they are working with and fear their intentions. In contrast, fishermen tend to see other men as essentially good, competent and interactive. On the Sentence Completion Test, in answer to the stub "men," the cutters spoke of the unkindness they felt in others. The fishermen spoke of the positive side: "is good at this earth"; "two or three work together"; "as a whole should unite with one another and social life"; "am kind—is very good to each one another." Because the fishermen feel this way they are able to work together on a basis of relative trust and cooperation, without the need to suspect or harm one another. The responses of both groups to this stem are given in Table 7-9. Comparison of categories I and II shows a significant difference at the .01 level with the Fisher test.

Just as we found to be the case with the cutting gang, these principles are not an inexorable result of close contact of three men or an institutional requirement of a fishing crew. We shall meet in Chapter 8 a crew on an-

[6] If we wish to estimate the negative characteristics of leadership in the two occupations we may lump together categories II and III, and compare them against category I. This shows a significant difference between the groups at the .025 level with the Fisher test. If we wish to determine the helpful, cooperative or nurturant aspects of the leader, we may compare categories I and II against III. This yields a significant difference beyond the .005 level.

Table 7-9

Responses to sentence completion stem: "Men"

	Bad, Weak Take Advantage	Good, Competent, Interactive	Neutral
Fishermen	3	10	2
Cane Cutters	11	3	2

other island which structures itself on a strongly authoritarian rule with a lack of integration among the fishermen.

Instability of Crew. Yet one of the most striking features of fishing in Dieppe Bay is the great frequency with which crews break up and re-form. Scarcely a week goes by without a major quarrel in one of the boats, and it is rare for a crew to maintain the same membership throughout the year. This occurs so often that it must not be interpreted as merely discord within the crew, but rather as one of the fundamental principles of crew structure. This lack of stability in membership is one of the greatest weaknesses of the fishing crew. I should like to present several examples of conflict and then discuss the effects on the crew and the reasons for its occurrence.

For several weeks I noticed a great deal of contention in one boat composed of two older experienced fishermen and a young man with no pots, over what the men described as too great demands for "honor" on the part of the captain. Finally, the problem came to a head when the captain insisted that the older man sweep out his yard. He refused and in the ensuing dispute was fired/quit. For the next two weeks he walked around on the bay attempting to make some money casting a sprat net. He then worked sporadically as a spare hand on another crew for several weeks until he was able to gain a regular place. During this time the captain, who was short-handed, was forced to employ an inexperienced boy who had no fish pots. This breakup was neither of use to the captain nor the man. The captain was hurt because by adding another boy to the crew he lost all the advantage of experience previously discussed. The man, by refusing to submit to the captain's commands, forfeited his place in a successful crew. This captain, it must be noted, is considered by all the Dieppe Bay fishermen to be a basically good man. It is just that he has a "bad mouth" and says things that he regrets afterwards. Most of the men have worked with him at one time or another and all have had the same experience. Another man who left him because he was too quick-tempered put it this way: "he hasty and me hasty and two hasty people can't correspond."

A second incident occurred in a crew commanded by a very successful captain known as the most reasonable and considerate man on the bay. He took his crew net-fishing for bonito, and when his second man developed a headache at mid-morning brought him to shore. After letting him off the boat they continued fishing. When the catch was divided up the second received nothing—which went against a basic rule that a man taken ill will get an equal share. The second complained bitterly, in front of the people on the beach, that this was unfair treatment as he was the only dependable man the captain had. In retaliation for making an uproar he was fired. Later in the week, on a day when only a small sting ray was caught, the captain insisted on taking out a boat share. This is contrary to another rule that when only a small amount is caught the captain will forego the boat share. Again, a crewman, this time one who possessed no pots, objected in front of people. In retribution, the captain retorted that henceforth he would only take his son out to care for the turtle nets. This is a most interesting example of a captain's causing himself to lose his most productive men and being forced to rely on less and less competent people. In this case, not only was his son an inexperienced adolescent, but, it was said, he could not even stand up in a boat.

These examples teach a clear lesson. The captain's aggression is usually an attempt to gratify his need for self-esteem. He demands "honor" from the men by forcing them to do a menial task or humiliating his crewmen in some way to show that he is greater than they. This is quite irrational as the result is often loss of the crewman, with an immediate reduction in the efficiency of the boat. The significant factor for the break-up of the crew lies in the reaction of the crewman he is attempting to demean. In contrast to the cane cutter's response of complaints and acquiescence, the fishermen reply with no idle abuse. They challenge the captain openly and vociferously and either force him to change his ways or else leave him for a situation in which they will be more respected. They usually find something, which lasts until another clash over self-esteem forces the break-up of that crew. Only when a fisherman is desperate, without pot resources of any kind or the hopes of getting another job will he indulge the captain's humors.

I observed one such incident where a captain was sitting under a tree bracing a fish pot and joking with two other fishermen. When he finished he called his son to carry the tools and extra wood home. But as there was too much for the son to carry he commanded one fisherman, who was in this very weak position, to take up the rest. The man got up, put the sticks on his head muttering indignantly "You too fast, man. You too fast." [7] He had to accept a gross infringement of the code of conduct because he was so weak, but clearly felt the captain should have carried the sticks himself. With most other crewmen this would have caused the crew to break up. Conflicts such as these are expected. As one crewman put it, "If you don't own your own property a failure must come between you. Don't believe you going to stay with one man all the days of you life." Another explained this with a delightful phrase: "tongue and teeth must knock."

We have already seen the cane cutter's responses to the Projective Question "What happens if the man over you doesn't treat you right?" which was designed to bring out their attitudes to this issue. The fishermen tended to challenge the perpetrator and change the situation. A categorization of the responses, compared with those of the cutters already presented on page 91, is given in Table 7-10. Some examples of the fishermen's completions are given below.

[7] The word "fast," as it was used in this instance, means disrespectful.

"I'll tell him that he is not treating me the way he should."

"I would leave the job."

"Sometime it is only bad mind. I have to move from him—draw away."

"Well, that means he wants everything for heself and everyone else be damned. Leave him and go somewhere else to work."

As a group, the fishermen have satisfied their lower needs and can begin to function on the level of self-esteem. Both captain and men are extremely sensitive to slights and quick to take offense. From the point of view

TABLE 7-10

Responses to projective question: "What happens when the man over you doesn't treat you right?"

	Response is	
	Active	Passive
Fishermen	10	4
Cane Cutters	4	11

$p < .025$
(Fisher test)

of efficient crew organization, these men are too "hasty"; too quick both to give and receive insults. Because these unsatisfied needs are dominant, the crew is often in a constant uproar. Injury to self-esteem is the focal point of most conflicts in the crew, rather than the attempts at personal advantage which characterize the cane gangs, and shows the fishermen to be similar to the cane cutters of British Guiana we have discussed in Chapter 6. These offenses have much in common with the difficulty over "eye-pass." That the central conflict of a fishing crew can be similar to one in a cane gang in another area is a striking demonstration of the premise that much of the organization of an economic unit is determined by the particular psychological needs that must be gratified.

III. ROLES

A. *The Gar Boat Crew*

The dominant figure in the gar crew is the captain. Either he owns the boat and net or else he is approached by an owner and asked to work it for him for the season. It is the captain's obligation to hire the crew and direct all the fishing activities. He is also responsible both to the owner and to the police for the safety of the boat and crew. When I asked for the captain's responsibilities on the Interview I was invariably told that he is in full charge. Some of the men responded this way: He is responsible

> "for the men. In any accident he has to tell the government. If men fight, captain will go to the [police] station."
> "for your life"
> "for everybody. Must teach them everyday what to do."
> "Everything after moving from the land. See everything be in order."
> "Safety of crew and boat and the efforts to make a good catch."

The captain must keep track of the seasons, tides, and fishing locations and has the authority to command where the boat will search for gar. He is also in charge of training the crewmen and often will spend a good deal of time teaching the second man how to shoot the net. This is to his advantage because if he gets sick for a day the second can handle the boat. Most important, it is his duty to shoot the net and guide the men's efforts in encircling the school of fish and hauling the heavily laden net into the boat.

When the boat reaches shore after a day's fishing, the captain jumps out and waits for the men to unload the net. After the gar are disentangled from the net and thrown together in the bottom of the boat, the captain, and no one else, proceeds to divide the catch. With a four-man crew he makes ten piles of fish by taking three or four fish of equal size at a time and laying them out on the sand. Each of the men gets one pile, the owner gets four and then the owner and crew divide one of the two remaining piles. Half of this last pile and the final pile of fish are distributed among the crewmen equally. All this time the men stand around the captain and watch as he shares out the catch. After the fish are divided the men, individually, give theirs to the women who take care of the selling for them.

After the fish have been given to the women who sell the fish ("sellers"), the captain directs the men in spreading the net over the beach to dry. The men are then free to go home to wash and eat their lunch. However, in the course of fishing the net often tears and requires mending, which is one of the most odious duties of both the captain and the men. To the men it means possibly sitting in the hot sun all afternoon, working for, what seems to them, no immediate return. Fishing is enjoyable because they earn money and have the excitement and challenge of successfully netting the gar. But mending is unproductive, unexciting, unpleasant, and tedious. Because of this the men try in every way to avoid their obligations, and when they desultorily do come out they are in a bad humor and complain bitterly.

Controlling the men in this activity is the duty of the captain. Not only must he set the example of mending earlier and longer than everyone else, he must corral the men and keep them under constant pressure to complete the job. Mending is so disliked that it is one of the major sources of friction in the crew. We have seen, earlier, that disinclination to assume responsibility for this work was one of the factors that broke up the "syndicate."

As I have mentioned, over half the men who staff the gar boats are full-time workers on the estates who only come down to the bay in the dull season. In many ways they resemble the cane cutters. They have no investment or commitment to fishing and are merely hiring on to the job. Only the captain, and occasionally the second, are full-time fishermen. The result of this kind of crew membership is to place a burden on the gar-boat captain similar to that borne by the head cutter. These men still want someone to take over-all responsibility and give direction to their efforts. They are not capable of providing their own initiative and must function as subordinates.

The role of captain is similar to the head cutter in that he must be the pace setter; he must rouse the men and have them on the beach on time; he must guide them at work; he must see to it that they mend the net; and he must regulate their conduct with each other at sea. Similarly, one of his main duties is to "encourage" the men, without which they become despondent and resentful. Typically, this takes the form of calling the men into the rum shop, occasionally, and standing a round of drinks. He must be continually enthusiastic and stimulate the men to greater efforts. As one fisherman phrased it: "the captain should say, 'OK boys, let's go.' "

If the captain does not fulfill these requirements the men will leave him. There was one gar crew, during the season I was in the village, which broke up because the men felt at a loss when the captain did not give this kind of direction. My records on gar fishing yields show that of the three boats one is doing quite well, another moderately well and the third very poorly. The difference can be explained by reference to the behavior of the various captains. The most successful crew is headed by an extremely aggressive and dedicated man, who energetically mobilizes his crew and forces them to work hard. He usually can be seen early in the morning and late in the evening walking around on the beach looking out to sea. When I spoke with him about it, he said that he was trying to figure out where the gar would be. It is not surprising that the most successful boat had the only captain who scanned the winds and tides carefully.

The moderately successful boat is led by a young man who is really a second, but is acting as captain for the season. He is an up-and-coming fisherman, though he still has not learned all the skills of commanding men and the ways of the sea.

The last captain, who did poorly during the season, is scorned as a lazy man. He has a lackadaisical attitude toward the work and refuses to command the men or give them the necessary direction. He is seldom seen on the bay and spends most of his time sleeping or in clean clothes in the rum shop complaining over his ill luck. His men sometimes, somewhat hopelessly, take his boat out without him in an effort to get him to "turn around faster," but they too have little luck without someone to guide them. The crew was virtually smashed after six weeks of operation when two of his men fell to quarreling over a fish head in a stew they were eating together, and one stabbed the other in the stomach. The injured man went to the hospital for two months and the other to jail for six. This is an extreme case of crew breakdown when there is no control by the captain.

In general, one need only watch their departures in the morning to recognize the more aggressive crew. The first boat consistently left before the others and returned to the beach last. The second was in an intermediate position. The captain of the third usually was seen in mid-morning walking around on the beach and watching the progress of the first two boats. If they seemed to be catching fish, he would call his men and go out. When he did go out, he was the first to get discouraged and the first to return.

B. *The Pot Fish Crew*

1. *The Basis for Prestige in the Crew.* As we have seen, the pot fish crew is an integrated unit of equals. Although there are two main positions, captain and men, in practice the respect which each man receives in the crew is not based on the position he occupies, as in the cutting gang. Rather, the opinion one fisherman holds of another is the result of that man's total behavior—both on land and sea.

We have seen examples of the cane cutter's reaction on page 103, and a comparison with those of the fishermen was presented in Table 5-1, which may be referred to for the full data. It is well, however, to examine some of the fishermen's responses in order to see the different basis upon which prestige rests.

"How you move with the person. Have to have manners."
"The ambition of the man. If he moves briskly. If he can be taught."
"The way he behaves on the land. His knowledge and sea experience."
"[if a] man work honest and faithful, if he act fair. Then will act like two brothers."

"The way you carry yourself. Don't knock about streets. No bad language."

"We are supposed to respect one another. Not just one man."

Fishermen, who are on a higher level of personality functioning, are able to respond to personal qualities in their fellows and can evaluate and relate to each other on this basis. This is not, in any way, a reflection of differences in power between the head cutter and captain. Actually, the captain has greater power over the men. He hires them and has complete authority to dismiss anyone he chooses, while the head cutter, in the end, can only complain to the estate manager and have the offender transferred. Yet, although the residual power is greater in the captain, only one fisherman went so far as to comment, "We doesn't give a damn about the boys underneath. We just studying the captain."

2. *Duties in the Crew.* The roles of the captain and the men in the pot fish boats are very different from those in other work groups we have examined. Full-time fishermen, even though they work in a crew, are autonomously operating workers. They are men who have invested in their own equipment and have a capacity and desire to have it yield a return.

To be sure there are duties which are uniquely the captain's responsibility. He owns or arranges for the boat, takes care of painting and repairs and guides the men in carefully washing the boat after each day's work. He takes charge by proposing a general plan for the day's operations, and as he is usually the most experienced man, he keeps track of the seasons and tides and advises the men where to set their pots. As the man who has organized the crew and has the greatest number of pots, he determines the general area in which the boat will fish. He also has specific duties in the crew. As the man in overall charge, he steers the boat to the fishing grounds and uses the water glass to search for all the men's pots. There are several further general duties which devolve upon him, such as deciding when it is propitious to go out and calling the men together on time. He acts as teacher to the less experienced, advising them on the lore of the sea and helping them to improve their skills. Finally, he keeps track of all the men's fishpots in order to help a man who is ill on a particular day.

But the ultimate responsibility for the success of a crewman does not rest in the captain. Each man is obliged to put money aside for fish pots. Each will build his own pots and, in his wisdom, decide where they shall be placed. A man must keep track of his own marks and arrange for his own customers. Whereas the captain of a gar boat divides the catch, a pot fisherman keeps his own in a separate place in the bottom of the boat. He, alone, divides his fish and gives the others their share. The individual fisherman's control over his own catch is evident in the principle that a crewman has a right to decide which of the fish he will share. For example, if he has a customer who prefers one species of fish, he has the right to select other species to place in the pool. If an especially large or attractive fish is caught the crewman is not obligated to share it at all.

We may conclude that this arrangement is determined by the personality of the fishermen for two reasons. First, it is conceivable that the captain could exert an authoritarian rule over the men, deciding where the pots shall be placed and the number of pots allowed to each man, taking charge of the division of the fish and arranging for the customers.[8] Second, if the majority of the men did not wish to become individually operating fishermen, they could merely hire on to the boat, work as a crewman and be compensated from the captain's catch. However, the fishermen of Dieppe Bay wanted to be independently operating workers when they left the estate, and therefore they have structured the crew to conform to their needs.

3. *Encouragement*. In general, each man in the crew is autonomous. Although all the men work closely together, each assuming specific aspects of the work and interacting for the same goal, sharing knowledge and intuition, the ultimate responsibility for their success is their own. We can see this in the different form "encouragement" takes in a gar boat and cutting gang on

[8] See Chapter 8 for an example of a fishing crew organized on this basis.

the one hand, and the pot boats on the other. In the cane gang and in the gar boat, the leader's job is to act as pace setter. He is obliged to keep the men at their work and prevent them from their "natural" inclination of slacking off. Encouragement, in this system, whether specific favors like drinks, inspiring words or threats is the leader's attempt to insure the continuation of the work.

The pot fishermen also speak of "encouragement," but for them it has an essentially different purpose. Basically, "encouragement" in the pot crew takes two forms. First, a captain must not set himself above the others or attempt to take advantage of them. Specifically, he should not be too boastful or try to make a man demean himself by forcing him to do menial labor for the captain. We have met this demand earlier and have seen how it is related to the need for self-esteem. Second, the captain must understand the problems facing a man. One major instance of this occurs when the boat returns home and the crewman has caught very little. On that day the captain is supposed to forgo his right to the boat's share, so the man can have something to take home to eat. Encouragement, then, is not an attempt to set the pace of the work group, for the pot fishermen are sufficiently motivated and have no need of an external regulator. What they have attempted to do is to shape the system to insure themselves against a very bad day and to preserve their self-esteem. A captain who does not fulfill this requirement is disliked and has difficulty getting a crew. There are several boats on the beach, at present, which were purchased by such men, who because their personal characteristics were "not encouraging" were unable to get a crew. The result is that they were forced to work with someone else, while their investment rotted on the sand.

4. *The Psychological Limitation on the Integration of the Crew.* One unfortunate result of comparing two groups is that "less good" and "more good" tend to be understood as the dichotomy of "bad" versus "good." It would be unjustified if the degree of solidarity and cooperation clearly evident in the fishermen's crew was seen as an example of total integration. I tried to temper

overstatement in the previous discussion of the "syndicate," when I attempted to demonstrate that cooperation on that level was beyond the fishermen's means. There are further developments possible which have not been established in the present fishing organization. I should like to mention a few to illustrate the limits set by the psychological capacities of these fishermen.

One might expect that when a fisherman has many of his pots swept away by the sea and does not have the financial resources to replace them, the other men in the crew, particularly the captain who is wealthy by their standards, would lend that man money or equipment. Yet this does not occur. Indeed, there seems to be a clearly articulated rule against expecting assistance from a fisherman who is better off. The men feel that the only way to possess equipment is through individual saving. Irreparable losses of this sort have driven several fishermen of my acquaintance from the bay. Another form this lack of solidarity takes is a general reluctance on the part of the experienced men to teach newcomers the trade. The men claim that this is because the men "grudge" others knowledge and success.

This can only work to the captain's or other experienced men's disadvantage. The captain is the loser because if he had well-trained men with many fish pots he would be repaid manyfold, as he could take his share of that man's catch. It is entirely within the captain's interest to have his men possess pots, not only for the increased share, but also because ownership of pots makes a man committed to making his living from the sea. The more a man is committed, and the more experience he gains, the more valuable he becomes to everyone in the crew. Another limitation is the occasional cursory searching or even outright refusal to look when a man's pot is lost. Although the captain demands that the boat must thoroughly search for his own missing pots, he sometimes is reluctant to make the same effort after his crewman's. Through this lack of consideration a beginner can lose all his fish pots. If a man feels that he cannot earn enough, or is driven away out of sheer need, he is forced to return to the estate.

Therefore, perhaps it is not only psychological forces

in most of the villagers that keeps them in the cane. Possibly, it is also the particular need level of the men with whom a newcomer would have to associate which makes it difficult for him to learn the trade and accumulate the necessary equipment to become a full-time man.[9]

Overview of Work Group Structure. The pot fishing crew completes the varieties of work group organizations I studied on St. Kitts. It is possible, if we examine them in relation to one another, from the viewpoint of need gratification, to order them all in a hierarchy of psychological functioning. Establishing a major continuum of the increased capacity for interaction and gratification of interpersonal needs, and the lessened need for safety, we may discover the following hierarchy:

> cutting gang
> broken cutting gang
> gar fishing crew
> pot fishing crew
> syndicate

The cane cutters, generally, have the lowest capacity for interpersonal relationships. The demands which a fishing crew makes are beyond their resources. Furthermore, as most of these men are at the safety level, the need for higher level structures has not yet significantly developed. Only those few who are on a somewhat more advanced level may create the broken cane cutting gang or enter the temporary structure of the gar crew. The fishermen, on the other hand, withdrew from cane cutting because they were unable to find their desired satisfactions on the estate. Concerned with deeper affectional relations and opportunities for gratifying their need for self-esteem, they have developed the pot fishing crew in its present form. We shall see in Chapter 8 that this crew design is not a necessary result of pot fishing, for there are fishing

---

[9] But I do not want to overstate my own cautions. Men, not only from the village, do become fishermen, do work well together, usually get the boat to look for their missing pots, and help each other to make fishpots. In the discussion above I am only concerned to describe certain of the forces working against the most ideally efficient crew.

crews on other West Indian islands which are similar in structure to the cane gang, as well as crews which are further advanced. Finally, the syndicate is the most advanced organization I discovered on St. Kitts. It was attempted by a group of fishermen, but necessitated a level of functioning far beyond their means.

IV. MARKETING OF THE FISH: CUSTOMERSHIP

The cane gang differs from the fishing crew in one fundamental respect. While the estate is a large stratified organization within which the gang performs a specialized task, the crew is a totality created by the men who engage in the work. It is necessary for the fishermen to form structures to carry out economic requirements which on the estate are handled by various other subsystems.

One of the most important of the systems left in the hands of the estate management is the means of disposing of their produce. The estate has a hierarchy of work units, which extend throughout the island and to Europe, engaged in weighing, transporting, refining and selling the sugar cane. Obviously, many of these tasks are not required for the relatively limited amount of fish caught in Dieppe Bay. However, it is essential for the fishermen to arrange for the marketing of their fish, which obligation finds no parallel among the cane cutters.

Although a small amount of fish is weighed and sold directly on the bay, the greatest part is put into the hands of women who do the selling for the men. There are three patterns of marketing in Dieppe Bay. Single men give their fish to one of the three women who work full-time at selling fish. They are forced to use these women, even though they generally do not catch a great quantity of fish, because they have no woman to dispose of it for them. Middle-range fishermen, those who catch on the average sixty pounds of fish a week, give their fish to their own women to sell. The large-scale fishermen, who may have one to three hundred pounds of fish each week, turn their catch over to one of these three professional "sellers." They give the "sellers" their fish because disposing of such a large amount is a full-time job, and their women, who generally seem to have very large families, do not have the time. The specific feature of the marketing system which has relevance for the general hypothesis under examination, is that all three of these patterns conform to one basic principle. Everyone, whether the fisherman's woman or the professional "seller," makes permanent arrangements with particular people (customers) in the village or in neighboring villages to take a fixed amount of fish whenever available. Very infrequently will their catch be sold on a "first come" basis. The more fish a woman has to dispose of the more customers she will take on. The number of customers the fishermen in my sample have ranges from four to thirty-four, all of whom are obligated to purchase one or two pounds of fish when available.

There are two kinds of customers: those who pay by the week and those who pay by the month. Records are kept of the amount of fish given to the "monthlies," who pay a large lump sum on the first of each month. These are, generally, government civil servants, such as nurses, who receive their own salaries by the month. This money is used by the fishermen to pay their big bills, e.g., for equipment. If a fisherman has caught little on a particular day he is obligated to buy fish from another man so he can meet these commitments.

Weekly customers do not have to buy the fish when it is sent to them and no record is kept on the quantity they buy. They have a prior call on the fish because the fishermen must pay their own weekly bills at the shop. It is interesting, from the point of view of self-esteem, that these people are required to come to the fishermen on Saturday to pay their bills. If they delay, or if the man has to ask them for the money, it is considered an unforgivable insult and the fisherman makes arrangements with another person.

Customership is emphatically not the result of fishermen protecting themselves against overproduction. We have seen, on page 43, that there is a large demand for fish which cannot be satisfied at the present level of production. Whatever amount is caught is sold within the hour and village women clamor for more.

The basis of customership, I propose, and the interest it holds for the theoretical problem, lies in the psychology of a village population which demands immediate gratifications and has trouble saving and budgeting money over a period of a week. This is a function of a modal personality trait expressing a need for safety. Pleasures have been so unreliable and frustration so frequent in the life of most Kittitians, that the typical individual tends to spend whatever money he possesses when he discovers a desirable object.

Evidence for this proposition comes from several sources. First, we have seen that as a whole the population of St. Kitts has a high mortality rate. Not only are many lost through illness, which shows up on mortality tables, but it is the unusual person who has not experienced the departure in childhood of someone close, either through emigration or desertion. Commonly, these blows to the family affect the basic nutritional level, as well as being a psychological loss. Virtually all the members of my sample, who are the most stable and productive workers in the village, have suffered relatively high losses by our standards. Second, from behavioral evidence the greatest number of people express difficulty in holding on to their money and mistrust their ability to withstand temptation. Even one of the most successful fishermen, explaining his preference for a system of customers, based his argument on the fact that if he earned a small amount of money each day he would be tempted to waste it on unnecessary articles. Receiving his money in a lump sum, weekly or monthly, thus enables him to pay off his large creditors.

Further proof of this self-mistrust can be seen in the use of pigs as a form of saving in the village. The people feed the pig daily, which costs them only a small amount of money, perhaps enough for several cigarettes and a drink. By the end of the year they can butcher the pig and gain a substantial sum. But that sum is usually less than what they have laid out in terms of food, and they run the risk of the pig falling ill and becoming a total loss. The pig, as a form of saving, is literally a piggy bank, utilized by people who have difficulty holding on to money. As Sidney Mintz (1964) has remarked, "It is hardly accidental that piggy banks are made to look as they do."

Functioning, therefore, in a social environment in

which the villagers have difficulty retaining money throughout the week, because of their psychological needs, a general pattern of short-term credit relationships is created. Most of the women establish a credit account at the shop and charge their purchases to their bills. On Saturday, when they are paid, they go to the stores and clear off their debts. It should be clearly understood that the credit system in Dieppe Bay is not designed to tide the villagers over several months of unemployment.

Because Dieppe Bay has a credit economy, and the fishermen have to extend credit, they tend to select the most reliable people in the village to trust. If they were to sell their fish on the beach on credit to all comers they would have to spend a good deal of their time collecting money, and many people would default. By instituting a system of "customers" the fishermen are confident that they will be paid for their fish with the least amount of trouble.

8

Comparative Materials
on the Fishing Crew

There are several studies of West Indian fishing communities to which we may turn for comparative materials, as it is necessary to show that there are no absolute requirements in the nature of fishing, as an economic institution, which demand the structures found in Dieppe Bay. Analysis of these studies shows that small-scale offshore fishing subcultures may be organized in ways which are quite dissimilar to those of Dieppe Bay. It is interesting to note that when fishing is organized in a different fashion the major psychological determinants, which I believe are important in influencing economic structure, vary in a similar manner. The congruence between these variables is a further demonstration of the explanatory power of the concepts I am proposing.

TWO JAMAICAN FISHING VILLAGES [1]

In this study Davenport presents an excellent and very thorough account of two Jamaican fishing villages.[2] One of these villages, Negril, is in many ways quite similar to the subculture of fishing in Dieppe Bay, and in some respects is an organization functioning on a higher psychological level. The other village, Farquhar Beach, is very different from Negril, and its culture appears to be parallel to that of the cane cutters. In both of the villages the major ecological and psychological

---

[1] Davenport, W. "A Comparative Study of Two Jamaican Fishing Villages." Unpublished Ph.D. dissertation, Yale University, 1956.

[2] Davenport discusses the technology of off-shore fishing at great length. Since much of Jamaican technology is identical with that utilized in Dieppe Bay, his work should be referred to by anyone interested in these aspects.

factors which have been found to be significant in determining the specific work group features of Dieppe Bay and the sugar estates on other Caribbean Islands are similarly found to exist.

Negril

This village is surrounded by large properties which take up all the good land in the area. Yet there is enough marginal land available for virtually all the inhabitants to own their houseplot as well as small pieces of land suitable for growing ground provisions. On the basis of a village survey Davenport found that only 4% of the households were landless and forced to rent land for house sites and cultivation. Of the households, 75% owned enough land not to have to rent any, 82% of the households owned more than one acre, with the average village holding between one and two acres. Davenport states, "Every house site has at least one or two crop producing trees, a few yam hills, some sugar cane, pumpkins, and some corn, or what might be called a kitchen garden." Beside the land which is owned and worked there is a good deal left entirely uncultivated.

Virtually all of the fishermen were born in Negril, and most of those not native to the village are women from nearby who have come in to live with Negril men. In general, Davenport found the village a place of "incomparable beauty" and the residents pleased with their village and rooted to their district. He summarizes their attitudes with the local remark: "Negril is a fine place, it only needs a little money."

Following the reasoning used throughout this work, the high degree of land ownership and the stability of the population may be interpreted as providing a good deal of satisfaction of the most basic needs. There is little problem of food, and ownership of land provides a general security from exploitation, establishes roots in a locality and yields a relatively stable family life, with the resulting gratifications of physiological, safety and love needs.

The economic organization of fishing functions equally on a high level. Most of the men work alone setting fish pots in their own cottonwood canoes. They assume full responsibility for their own efforts and thus yield none of the requirements of initiative and control. Davenport states that most of the men aspire to operate their own canoes, and since these are relatively inexpensive they are able to purchase one quite early in their careers.

In one section of the Negril District many of the men work together in two and three man crews. This is due to the small beach area in that section which curtails the possible number of canoes, plus the greater distance to the fishing grounds which makes it desirable to have assistance in paddling. These fishing crews are usually formed by friends or relatives. In these crews, formed by Negril fishermen, although there is some preference given to the man who owns the canoes, the crew functions as a group of equals. There is no emphasis on the role of captain, the owner assumes no responsibility for the efforts of the other men, and exerts no autocratic control over their activities. Interestingly, in light of the structure in Dieppe Bay, the men do not pool their catch or give the boat owner any of their fish. The assumption is that the rowing and company the other men give is sufficient compensation for the use of his canoe. If one man does not catch anything the others give him enough to eat. One mark of the democratic structure within these crews is the fact that the owners of the canoes do not set any limits to the number of pots a crewman may set. This is similar to the practice in Dieppe Bay, but is in great contrast to the situation in Farquhar Beach.

The recruitment process is described as a nurturant. Davenport claims that after a man has made a few pots of bamboo almost anyone will teach him the trade. Often he starts while he is still a dependent in his parental household.[3] A beginner always can find a place in a friend or relative's canoe. After he learns the trade, and amasses some capital he can buy wire pots and a canoe and strike out for himself.

The Negril fishermen set their pots throughout the fishing grounds and feel free to place them close to those

[3] Recall that fishermen in Dieppe Bay seldom learn their trade from their fathers. The occurrence of this in Negril is an interesting indication of deeper, less conflicted, father-son ties.

of another man. This results in the pots becoming thoroughly intermingled with those of all the other Negril fishermen. In general, these men do not fear that the fish in their pots will be stolen, make no special efforts to detect if their pots have been raised by another man and are free with the information they possess of the fishing trade. All these arrangements, as well, are similar to Dieppe Bay and in contrast to Farquhar Beach.

In Negril there are three crews of six to ten men who operate a large seine, 175 feet long. As in gar fishing in Dieppe Bay, this entails intensive and integrated cooperation. The men use three or more small canoes and must coordinate their efforts to drive the fish into the central "bag." The psychological requirements for this kind of work have already been discussed (p. 123). Although a pattern of cooperation exists to this degree, the seine is always owned by a single individual. Davenport reports no instances where several men jointly own and operate a seine, as the Dieppe Bay fisherman attempted with their "Syndicate."

However, there are two kinds of joint activity in Negril not found in either Dieppe Bay or Farquhar Beach. The first is the collective ownership of brail nets by two or three fishermen. These small casting nets are used to catch the sprats and fry with which Negril men bait their fish pots. This is the only successful example of joint ownership in fishing I have come across in the West Indies. The second instance is a pooling arrangement to dispose of some of the fish. A good many Negril fishermen, including all the seine operators, take a substantial amount of their catch to a market twelve miles away. They form pools of six to eight fishermen, and, whenever there is a surplus, three to four men take the entire catch caught by the pool to the market.

Farquhar Beach

Farquhar Beach is a fishing community of great contrast to both Dieppe Bay and Negril. The economic arrangements which have developed provide a clear example of the possibility of organizing a fishing crew on the basis of safety needs.

The village is on a 30-acre strip of land sandwiched in between a steep hill, a mangrove swamp and a narrow sand beach. The land was rented as a whole from the estate by one man known as the "Captain," who has contracted for the exclusive right to manage all residential, wholesale, retail, fishing and agricultural activities which may take place. He pays the estate for this privilege and in turn has a free hand to extract whatever gain is possible. To the residents, Davenport states, he is the "Lord and Master of Farquhar Beach."

All the land for the house sites, as well as land for small agricultural plots must be rented from him. The fishermen must pay him one shilling per month for the use of the land and still another for the right to use the beach for the canoes. They are entirely at his mercy as he can put them off the land, if he desires, or cut off their credit at the one shop in the village, which he owns. Since he is the sole source of supplies, he adds an extra 10-15% interest on credit extended. When the boats come in, the Captain, or one of his cronies acting as his agent, will meet them and extract a few of the best quality fish from every basket as his tribute. This is over and above the monthly fee paid for the use of the beach, and the amount he takes from all 20 boats yields the Captain almost the equivalent of two thirds of a day's catch just in extortion.

In contrast to the fishermen of Dieppe Bay and Negril, only 25% of the population was born in the village. Over half migrated from St. Elizabeth Parish within the twelve years preceding Davenport's study and form a separate group within the village. The fact that over 75% of the population is new to the village, together with the inability to benefit from owning land, set in the general situation of exploitation and insecurity resulting from having to rely on the whims of a single man, produces a psychological environment which cannot satisfy the basic needs for safety.

The deprivations of primary needs are seen in several other facts presented by Davenport. Farquhar Beach has a problem with its drinking water. There is none in the village, and as it is difficult to collect the run-off from a roof of thatch it is necessary to bring in water from far away. Furthermore, this is a malarial area. All the people suffer from malaria, and every fisherman misses a day or two each month because of chills and fever. The cure is a cup of tea made with the marihuana they grow surreptitiously.

The basic form of fishing organization is a three- or four-man crew working in a large sailing canoe. The primary reason for this arrangement is ecological, as the boats must sail a great distance to reach the fishing grounds. The sea area they cover is 16 times larger than that of Negril, and on some days the men may row 30 miles.

Within this crew the internal structure is very different from Dieppe Bay's. The need for a large crew is set by environmental features of the area, like the crews of Negril and Dieppe Bay. But the internal structural arrangements vary, and are therefore determined by the psychological needs of the fishermen. The captain of the boat is a figure of much greater power. He decides where all the fish pots are to be set, including all the pots owned by the men in his crew. He is also charged with the responsibility for finding and raising all of the pots. The canoe captain is given great prestige because he occupies that position. In this respect he is very similar to the head cutters in Dieppe Bay. Every non-captain always addresses him by his title, "Captain," both on land as well as on sea. Within the village the captains form a special elite class. In contrast, Dieppe Bay captains are deeply involved in all the leisure-time activities and are addressed by their nicknames on sea as well as on land.

The captain has the power to limit the number of fish pots for each crewman, and can even determine if the man will set any at all. This is an aspect of crew structure completely foreign to Dieppe Bay, where crewmen are encouraged to set many pots. The crewmen who have no pots, furthermore, have not established a fixed share of the captain's catch for their own wage. The amount the man receives ranges from 1/7 to 1/10 of the captain's catch, depending on the amount the captain believes he is worth. This lack of a fixed wage principle is a great lever of control in the hands of the captain. In Negril, by contrast, a man without pots gets 1/4-1/5 of the captain's catch. In Dieppe Bay, the men receive 1/6-1/8 of the total catch, which includes fish from pots of the other men in the boat. In Farquhar Beach, a crewman does not get any fish from the other men's catch, a fact which, in itself, is quite revealing. It implies that the men working in a boat in Farquhar Beach are not really a crew, in the sense of an integrated group, functioning together for a common purpose. In structure, then, this seems to be similar to the cane gang of Dieppe Bay, where the main structural lines exist only between head cutter and each of the men separately. In the Farquhar Beach crew, they exist between the captain and the individual man.

We may speculate that this existing structure is due to an inability on the part of the Farquhar Beach fishermen to challenge the authority the captains usurp. This failure I have postulated lies at the heart of the cane gang structure, and the capacity for challenging authority is one of the factors creating the democratic structure of the Dieppe Bay crew. For certain, it is not due to any surplus of fishermen, for Davenport makes quite clear that there exists a great shortage of fishermen in Farquhar Beach, as well as in Negril. As I have already stated, there is also a shortage of fishermen in Dieppe Bay. Yet, whereas the same shortage of labor is found in all villages, a relatively democratic structure has developed in Dieppe Bay and Negril, and an authoritarian one has come about in Farquhar Beach.

Davenport cites four cases in which the men struck against their captain in Farquhar Beach.

1. The captain became involved in gambling and did not go out for a week. He also refused to let the men take the boat out.
2. The captain went on a two-week drunk and refused to let the men take the boat out.
3. The captain refused to spend money on badly needed repairs.
4. An old captain's eyesight failed so badly he could not see the landmarks for the pots and therefore could not find the pots.

In all cases the men pleaded with the captain to return to work, and in the last case they asked him to let them appoint an assistant to find the marks. Davenport seems to feel that these strikes were unusual and brought on by desperation. In any case, usually the captains will band together and refuse to hire any of the striking fishermen—and so force them back to work. These strikes are over very different kinds of issues from those in Dieppe Bay; these strikes are over simple physiological needs—the captain deprived the men of their entire income. In Dieppe Bay, as we have seen, arguments, strikes and resignations occur over incidents on the level of self-esteem. It is the crewman's ability to make this threat which raises his position in the crew and leads to an integrated group.

In several other respects, Farquhar Beach provides an example of one extreme end of the range of possibilities for organizing a fishing crew. The recruitment system, or the road traveled to become a full-fledged master fisherman, is again different from Dieppe Bay and Negril. In Negril there is positive encouragement to become a fisherman, while in Diepppe Bay there is a general attitude of tolerant neutrality. In Farquhar Beach, on the contrary, the captains do everything possible to keep a man in the dependent position. Not only do they refuse to lend him equipment and advice, they try hard to keep him from buying fish pots of his own by controlling the number he may set from the boat. A man must become very essential to the captain before he is allowed to set even a few pots. In this way it is virtually impossible for a working hand to accumulate sufficient money on his salary to buy enough pots to strike out on his own. It is interesting to note that the captains' negative attitude truly acts against their interest. As in Dieppe Bay, every year men come in from the sugar estates hoping to become fishermen. In Dieppe Bay, they are, to some extent, welcomed by the captains and men, and with money they have saved up in the cane they buy several pots and can start an economically productive life. In Farquhar Beach, they meet great difficulty, set in their way by the captains, and many leave fishing to return to their former pursuits. And still there is a shortage of fishermen!

I believe it is the events experienced in both their childhood and adult life which produce a group of men functioning on psychologically diminished levels of existence. In many ways these people are similar to the cane workers of Dieppe Bay. This clearly can be seen in one frequent form of crew arrangement in Farquhar Beach. A man will purchase pots and a boat and give it all out to a captain to run on a 50% share basis. The owner takes all the risks and responsibilities, and the captain as well as the men assume none. This types of arrangement encompasses from 23% to 36% of the total crews on the beach. Furthermore, 22% of all the fish pots set in the village are owned by other people who give them to fishermen on 50% shares. This is the height of a flight from responsibility, for if the men could assume this burden, they would wish to get as much return as they could from the few pots they are allowed to set.

It is interesting that in this village Davenport did not find any crews fishing with large seines. It is difficult to say if the lack of seine fishing is due to the captain's failure to assume that level of responsibility, or due to the crewmen's inability to function as an integrated crew. Possibly both factors are involved. What is clear, however, is that the lack of seine fishing is some function of the needs of the Farquhar Beach fishermen. We may be confident in this conclusion because other men from other villages frequently do come to seine fish in Farquhar Beach fishing grounds. Significantly, one of these visiting seine crews is owned by a man from Negril and captained by his son.

In general, the lack of integrated crew structure extends beyond the crew to encompass all the fishing activities of the village. The men are extremely fearful of theft and have developed a code of secrecy and suspicion. Each man laces his fish pot closed in a very special way so that he can detect if it has been wrongfully opened. They never jointly purchase brail nets as do the Negril fishermen. The captains keep the marks of the pots hidden even from the men in their crews, because they fear that they will give the information to other crews. Finally, in contrast to the practice on Dieppe Bay and Negril where all pots are set intermingled with those of the other men, the fishermen of Farquhar Beach have divided the fishing area up into separate areas, and each man must be careful not to set his pots in a section another fisherman is working. If a man is seen in another's area then it is assumed that he is stealing fish.

9

The Family

In previous chapters we have examined the way these men have organized their economic activities, and we now turn to view the processes which determine the structure of their social life. As we explore the principles which guide their most intimate contacts with other human beings, we are able to understand those features of the social organization which are the conditions by which their most pressing needs are met.

I. THE GOALS OF LEGAL
AND COMMON-LAW MARRIAGE

The contrast between legal and common-law marriages has been a topic of great concern in West Indian research. Discussion has centered on the meaning of the sharp divergence from the Western pattern: the instability of the family; non-legal unions; the high illegitimacy rate and the prevalence of what seemed to be casual matings. Recently, a consensus has been reached that the various forms make sense in their own terms; and attention has turned to such questions as the economic pattern and the family's relationship to the larger cultural system. The concern has been to determine the basic conditions the people face, and to relate these social institutions to the process of coming to grips with these problems.

In Dieppe Bay this same plurality of mating forms exists side by side. The analysis of these forms, and the conditions which have led to their creation, reveals a further determinant, which has not yet been discussed in the literature. Just as recent studies have shown the dependence of legal marriage on the particular form of economic activity (Clarke, 1957), in the case of

161

Dieppe Bay it may be seen as an institution developed largely to satisfy a psychological need.

In previous chapters I have discussed the personality structure of the fishermen and cane cutters and have shown how their economic activities are organized to satisfy their psychological needs. The pressure for gratification, which we have seen in operation in the economic sphere, also exerts its strong influence on the forms of the family as well. It is the purpose of this chapter to describe some of the most important aspects of these social structures in Dieppe Bay and determine the extent to which they are a function of the psychological needs of the members.

The most striking characteristic of the family in the sample of men I studied is the sharp differential in mating patterns. If we take a matched age group of men, 30-48 years of age,[1] we see that whereas most of the cane cutters are legally married, the fishermen, on the contrary, establish common-law unions. Of this age group, seven of nine cutters are legally married and six of eight fishermen have common-law marriages. See Table 9-1.

[1] It is necessary to establish a matched age group for the following reasons. In this sample, among the married men the youngest fisherman is thirty-one years old, while there are three cane cutters in their early and middle twenties. Various studies in the West Indian literature (Blake, 1961, M. G. Smith, 1962) have shown a sequence of mating relationships which follows the order of the solitary state, casual matings, common-law marriage, legal marriage and, once again, the solitary state. In this pattern common-law marriages are the first stable family arrangement men enter. These are followed, later on in life, when there is a lessening of the man's ability as a worker, by legal marriage. The increasing age of the man, at a time when his children are beginning to work and contributing money for their mother's support, makes him more dependent upon the woman and so he agrees to a legal marriage. Because men later on in life tend to get legally married in general, it seemed wise from the point of view of testing this hypothesis to limit the sample of men to the vigorous adult workers. If we include these two confounding elements, young cane cutters (who may yet become fishermen) and the older men who have a special, though extraneous, reason for legal marriage, the same trend as noted before is evident in the entire sample, although it does not quite reach the .05 level of significance.

TABLE 9-1

Mating pattern and occupation for the matched group

	Type of Marriage	
	Legal	Common Law
Fishermen	2	6
Cane Cutters	7	2
		$p < .05$ (Fisher test)

If the systems of legal and common-law marriage are contrasted, as they emerged from formal and informal interviewing, certain principles appear which shed a good deal of light on the functions they were created to serve. A common-law union fulfills many basic requirements: it establishes a means of economic cooperation, in which the man provides the greatest part of the money, and the woman takes charge of the domestic necessities; it legitimizes the relationship of the children to both parents, and insures their support; it provides for exclusive sexual, economic and domestic rights between partners—though with lesser demands in the case of the man; and it is a means for satisfying their need for intimacy. However, common-law unions do not formally establish rights to each other's property, or formally require mutual aid in times of crises. Some individuals claim that their partners share equally in all possessions and that they have full confidence in their assistance in an emergency. But this is a personal determination, not inherent in the social sanctions of the relationship. In general, it is an association whose value and continuation depends largely upon the degree of personal rapport existing between the members. One of its main features, after all, is the ease with which it may be ended.

In Dieppe Bay, legal marriage not only serves many of these functions, but also seems to be overlaid with extra provisions satisfying the men and women in different ways. These are derived from the following sources which may be summarized briefly before discussing each in detail. Some of these provisions stem from the British legal code, adapted to their own needs. Others evolve by assuming certain characteristics of the dominant English and English-oriented classes. Through acquisition of this form a link, however tenuous, is made with the "upper classes," and therefore yields a feeling of greater personal value vis-à-vis the rest of the laboring class. The final group of extra benefits, marking legal apart from common-law marriage, was structured by the villagers, as the provisions they were able to acquire from external sources were not sufficient for the needs which had to be met.

From the woman's point of view, legal marriage is a more satisfactory arrangement materially, as the law may be invoked to permit her to share and inherit her husband's possessions. It also compels the man to give her money; and if she is in trouble, he is responsible for her. Their children also benefit because some professions are open to them, which are closed to "bastards." For example, the Methodist theological seminaries will take only children of legitimate birth.

A legally married woman is considered more respectable and is more esteemed in the village. People speak more politely to her and she may assume the special title of "Mistress" or "Mrs." instead of the designation "Miss" reserved for the unmarried. Undoubtedly, this aura has a circular result, as it is a further reason for her husband to respect her. Finally, matrimony is viewed by most women as the proper state in the eyes of God, while common-law unions are felt to be sinful. Although not a burning issue which generates much guilt, the doctrine spread by the Protestant missionaries is unquestioningly accepted. In this, as in many other areas of religious dogma, the position the church takes is held to be self-evident. However, because so much of the church's teachings are irrelevant to the needs of the community, the doctrines do not deeply affect their behavior. The holiness of matrimony is, therefore, a limited, although quite real, extra inducement.

The obligations of the man to the woman in legal marriage have been elaborated above and beyond what is required by laws or demanded as part of the British value system. It is in these special externalized rules and sanctions that the proposed theoretical hypothesis exerts an extra power of explanation. It could be argued that the villagers do not selectively choose from a variety of possibilities according to their needs, but are merely opting for one of several cultural possibilities. However, the institutionalization of new forms demonstrates the strength of psychological needs to develop and add to the cultural material made available.

When married, a man is expected to take better care of his wife and is required to give her money for clothes, food, and all the household necessities. He must protect her from others and be responsible for her in case she falls ill. These are not legal compulsions, promulgated in London or in the Legislative Council of St. Kitts. Rather, these are rules and special inducements which they, themselves, institute to make the union more attractive for the woman, and which the community attempts to enforce. The institutionalization of support frees the woman of these worries and relieves her of the necessity to look to other men for money.

The man, on the other hand, values legal marriage because the external supports built into it help insure its long-term continuation. While a common-law marriage can be abrogated in a moment, a legal marriage is more difficult to dissolve. Because divorce is a lengthy and costly procedure, legal marriage, based on the external political system, insures gratification of the need to be involved in stable structures. Furthermore, under the judicial system the husband may prosecute his wife's partner in the case of adultery and receive heavy damages. This serves to frighten other men away from his wife and so helps to preserve the union. A man living in a common-law relationship does not have this power. Last, under the law a wife is responsible for her husband's burial; a keeper (common-law wife) is not.

According to the rules developed in this community, in times of trouble a wife is expected to stay with the man, while a keeper may ease herself from the burden. In general, a wife is expected to stay with her husband; a keeper is under no compulsion to remain with the man if she finds a better arrangement with another. Also, the people feel that while a wife can be trusted, a common-law partner will repeat confidences, gossip and expose the man to the rest of the village.

In summary, the benefits the woman receives from legal marriage are primarily material. Through the use of certain provisions from the British legal code and by the act of the villagers themselves, legal marriage insures support for the woman. The benefits to the man, however, are not essentially material. In this system of legal marriage, as opposed to common-law, he has been anxious to institutionalize the stability of his relationship with the woman. To achieve this he has had to grant her extra rights to his possessions, and in return she is bound to him and expected to remain with him through all difficulties. Most of the structure of legal marriage, then, is created to satisfy the needs of those men who are unsure of their own abilities and who, in psychological terms, have a special need for safety. In contrast, the common-law union does not present such institutionalized aids for the maintenance of the union. It is the result of those who are drawn together for affective and economic reasons and who, at the same time, have some confidence in their powers to continue the relationship. They are not seeking special precautions for gratifying an unsatisfied need for stability.

The dissimilarity in the mating pattern within the two occupational groups residing in the same village, combined with our knowledge of the differential gratifications inherent in legal and common-law marriage, indicates the extent of which social organization may be determined by the needs of its members. This has been seen in the relationship between occupational group and mating form presented in Table 9-1. It is now our obligation to explore this relationship more deeply and search for evidence which would confirm the explanations suggested.

1. Childhood Experience and Form of Mating

Since legal marriage is a system of externally institutionalized obligations and sanctions which, I propose, has been created to establish a more firm sense of order in the mating relationship, it is necessary to examine the particular life history of the individuals directly involved in order to determine if they have experienced events of such magnitude as to produce greater need for stability. It must then be shown that those who establish common-law relationships have had a more secure childhood and have had their need for safety satisfied.

As we have seen in Chapter 4, in determining the causes of occupational choice, the area of experience which would have the greatest impact on the individual's need for security is the stability of his primary family ties. Now we must consider the association of childhood experiences to the mating pattern. In Table 9-2 is presented

TABLE 9-2

Mating pattern and degree of loss for the matched group

Degree of Loss	Type of Marriage	
	Legal	Common-Law
High Loss	7	1
Low Loss	2	7
		$p < .025$ (Fisher test)

the relationship between mating forms and degree of loss suffered in childhood for the matched age groups. In this comparison high and low loss are defined by the same criteria used previously in Table 4-6. The present analysis should be seen as a more conclusive test of the proposed hypothesis, as childhood experience, rather than occupational category, is the critical determinant of this form of social structure.[2]

[2] For the sample of married men as a whole, including the two confounding elements, the relationship is even more significant ($p < .01$). Twelve of fourteen high loss men are legally married, and nine of thirteen low loss men are in common-law unions. This is due to the fact that occupation and degree of loss are not perfectly correlated, and there is a small number of men whose childhood experience runs counter to the predicted direction.

Those individuals who have undergone the greatest privations are those whose need for stability is most unsatisfied. Losses of this magnitude leave him without trust in his power to establish lasting relationships, for experience has demonstrated the shattering result of interpersonal bonds, as well as his complete helplessness to prevent the loss of those he loves. This is why legal marriage has become a structure of rules, restrictions and special inducements, all designed to insure, or at least enhance, the continuation of that relationship. Since one who has an unsatisfied need for stability does not have confidence in his own powers, this pattern of mating becomes a formalized system, in which he borrows many specific details of English law and marriage customs. Because he cannot maintain a system based on personal understandings, or even stand up to the strain of personal encounters, the system is based on external supports and justifications. The total institution combines these elements, quiets his fears and provides the means to achieve some gratification of unfulfilled primary needs.

Those who have enjoyed a more secure childhood have had their safety needs much more satisfied. They contemplate their present interpersonal attachments with much greater equanimity and find it unnecessary to elaborate structures guaranteeing the continuation of the relationship. Their concern in mating goes beyond the question of continuation, which is a matter of little moment and as an issue seems to be irrelevant.

When the safety needs of the members are unsatisfied the organization of mating is focused on that problem and its development is arrested. By development I refer to the fact that an institution created by these individuals is limited to solving only one basic task. As their psychological potentialities are set free, the structure of the family is freed as well and becomes concerned with other tasks. In Section II, I shall examine in detail the type of mating system brought about when the need for safety has been satisfied. Here I shall only note that those who have had a more secure childhood do indeed have a different form of mating.

However, this interpretation might be challenged on the grounds that, in contrast to the fishermen, many of the cane cutters were born on neighboring islands, which have a higher degree of marriage than St. Kitts. Although high loss determines who becomes a cane cutter, the incidence of marriage among cane cutters, it might be argued, is not surprising, as they are simply retaining those customs of their "native" land. Therefore the correlation between marriage and high loss would be an artifact of another, non-relevant, relationship.

This alternative explanation must be carefully considered, for otherwise the correlation would be dull and uninteresting. The critical test is to examine the relationship between loss and mating forms for those born on St. Kitts. If those men who have experienced a similar history and tradition produce dissimilar mating patterns on the basis of degree of childhood loss, then we are able to dismiss this reservation. According to its logic no distinction in the form of mating should be determined by severity of loss when there is no difference in past customs, and a random distribution would be predicted. Table 9-3 presents the results of this test.

TABLE 9-3

Mating pattern and degree of loss for those born on St. Kitts

Degree of Loss	Type of Marriage	
	Legal	Common-Law
High Loss	8	2
Low Loss	1	7
		$p < .01$ (Fisher test)

The data clearly disprove the possibility that the relationship between loss and mating is an artifact as argued.[3] For those born into the same historical tradition —those born on St. Kitts—mating forms are specifically

[3] I do not present separately the data for those not born on St. Kitts because of the small numbers of fishermen who are not native Kittitians, and the few cutters with low loss. To the extent that data are available, the argument is supported.

correlated to the degree of childhood loss. Those Kittitians with high loss are legally married, and those with low loss are in common-law relationships. Legal marriage is, therefore, not a reflection of the local customs of those from foreign islands, and its prevalence in St. Kitts is a direct function of the particular needs of the inhabitants—whether native born or not.

2. Emigration and Form of Mating

So far I have primarily sought to find the origins of safety deprivations in childhood experiences. If dynamic psychology has demonstrated anything at all, it is the power of childhood events to produce lasting personality states. But, it is also true that there are many significant factors in the adult environment which exert strong influences on personality as well.

Some of the most important questions we ask an informant are simple ones: Where were you born? When did you come here? These are asked as a matter of course —sometimes only to keep a conversation from stumbling. Primarily they are questions of orientation, which give many clues as to areas of information the person might be expected to know.

It is most interesting to wonder at the psychological meaning of the answers I received. Not so much as to why these people came here—if they were born outside the village—as to the effect on the men of entering a strange village; for they have had to give up their old ties and enter into the gamut of human relations as an alien. They must seek jobs from men who do not know them and are not known by them. They must work with a new group of men—rather than boyhood friends and acquaintances, which would have been the case if they had remained home, or were native to the village. As newcomers they have no friends, allies, relatives or people obligated to their families to rely on. They have no knowledge of which piece of mountain land to rent from the estate; they have difficulty in getting credit in the stores; and less assurance of being employed during the dull season. In general, they are ignorant of the people, jobs, short cuts, and angles, which all go to make life in a village somewhat easier. Finally, as we have seen in

Chapter 7, because they are strangers they draw many of the tensions and hatred of the village.

The state of being a permanent stranger is one of the most important situational variables I have discovered, and seems to exert a strong influence in the determination of the mating form. In this chapter, I have proposed that legal marriage is an institution specifically oriented to handle the main problem of deprived safety needs. To this point I have discussed events of childhood as either satisfying or depriving this basic need. Migration, in its very nature, is a phenomenon which causes uncertainty and produces a situation in which the individual, irrespective of events in his childhood, becomes insecure.

Therefore, we might expect that those who were not born in the village, having greater needs for safety, would try to compensate by creating security-satisfying structures. Table 9-4 presents the relationship between birthplace and mating pattern for the sample.

TABLE 9-4

Mating pattern and birthplace

Birthplace	Type of Marriage	
	Legal	Common-Law
Born in Dieppe Bay	2	6
Born outside Dieppe Bay	14	6
		$X^2 = 3.07$
		$p < .05$

There is a clear correlation between in-migration and the form of mating. The adult situation exerts its own influence and contributes to the basic motives that underlie legal marriage. Migration is another factor, which together with those previously mentioned, promotes a feeling of instability.

The power of migration to produce feelings of insecurity is further evident in the life histories of the women of the men in my sample. From the data gathered on the Female Interview a similar pattern to that of the

TABLE 9-5

Birthplace and mating pattern of women

Birthplace	Type of Marriage	
	Legal	Common-Law
Dieppe Bay	7	10
Outside of Dieppe Bay	7	1
		$p < .05$ (Fisher test)

men was found. We can see from Table 9-5 that those women who were born outside of Dieppe Bay choose to marry legally, while those born in Dieppe Bay tend to have common-law unions.

The choice of legal marriage for the Dieppe Bay women is not yet clear: the reason for this is seen in Table 9-6. Mating is an act of two people, and if we

TABLE 9-6

Mating pattern and birthplace of spouse, for the women born in Dieppe Bay

Birthplace	Type of Marriage	
	Legal	Common-Law
Man from island	1	8
Man from off-island	6	2
		$p < .025$ (Fisher test)

forget the motives of the partner a great deal of distortion can occur. Often, by shifting our focus to the other partner, it is possible to understand processes that seem unclear and to derive additional proof for our argument. Therefore, if we consider only those women who have been born in Dieppe Bay and examine the origin of their men, the meaning of their choice of mating pattern becomes apparent. When a woman from Dieppe Bay mates with a man born on the island a common-law relationship is set up; when she mates with a man born on another island a legal marriage is created. This accounts for the large number of legally married women born in Dieppe Bay. In other words, the principle of the psychological effects of migration operates equally in men and women. When they mate the most primary need becomes dominant. Migration produces insecurity, and, irrespective of sex, is one of the main determinants which establishes the form of mating.

It is here that one of the main values of the general theoretical approach I am proposing is most evident. Without a commitment to the study of psychological processes the meaning of a major influence on the form of the culture would have been lost. Migration would have been seen as one of many demographic "facts," but would not have been considered a "factor."

3. Relative Age of Mates

Another demographic fact whose significance is frequently overlooked is the relative age of the partners of the union. To the extent that age has been studied in the West Indian literature, it is used as a criterion for the movement in the social structure from one form of mating to another. For example, there is the previously discussed progression from solitary to common-law unions to legal marriage as the function of the individual's increasing age. This, of course, does not attribute any particular causal influences to a person's age, but merely states that age is correlative to a particular type of social unit.

When I included a question concerning the age of the mates of the members of my sample, as with the inquiry into birthplace, I primarily sought to establish the basic demographic facts in order to create a framework of orientation for my more general purposes. But, once again, when I found that fishermen and cane cutters were in different age positions vis-à-vis their mates, I again had a fact which demanded an explanation. This difference in relative age is presented in Table 9-7.

The fact that fishermen mate with women younger

TABLE 9-7

Occupation and relative age of women

	Relative Age of Women	
	Younger	Older
Fishermen	11	2
Cane Cutters	7	9

$p < .05$
(Fisher test)

than themselves, while a majority of cane cutters have women who are older than they,[4] is so striking a reversal of relative age positions that it leads beyond mere age data and opens an entirely new dimension of family structure. Again, because this result was unexpected, I began to wonder about its implications and started to use it as a leading question in the informal talks which are the heart of field work. The consensus reached might be summarized in an exchange I noted down with one informant.

> J.A. "Which is better, an older woman or a younger woman?"
> Informant. "A younger woman."
> J.A. "Why is that?"
> Inf. "You can play with her, but an older woman wants to go to sleep."
> J.A. "Any other reasons?"
> Inf. "An older woman is cranky, a younger one has a better nature—more fun. You can make jokes with her." (He then cited an example of two people whose ability to get on well together and make jokes he admired.) "If you have an older woman you have to find an outside girl to play with."
> J.A. "Why do people marry an older woman?"
> Inf. "Well, they say they do for them."

From these talks emerged a clear-cut difference as to the reasons why a younger or older woman is preferred. A

[4] The women average 5.1 years older than their men, with a range of 1-12 years, and a median of 6 years.

younger woman is seen as more of a companion. She is someone who is more affectionate, playful, and fun. She is capable of enjoying jokes, dances, drink and going on outings. She is more understanding and sympathetic than the older woman, who is seen as cranky and inflexible. She is also more of a sexual partner. ("You can play with her, but an older woman wants to go to sleep.") The older woman does not have these qualities, but she makes up for it by possessing other, antithetical, capabilities. She is an experienced housekeeper, and does not make too great emotional demands on the man. The men who desire her do not wish for love, which, indeed, is sometimes frightening to them; rather, they have a superordinate need to be taken care of. They want someone who is fully trained in all the details of running the house ("they say they *do* for them"). The word "do" is often heard, and has the somewhat archaic English connotation of "to cook and keep house."

The psychological reasons underlying the difference in relative age of the partner were clearly presented on the Sentence Completion Test. Two stems, "A woman older than me," and "A woman younger than me," were included in hopes of tapping these attitudes. Most of the responses to this question brought rather neutral material, i.e., "A woman older than me . . . is my mother," "A woman younger than me . . . is my sister." Those responses, which contained information related to this problem, came mostly from men with older women or from solitary men. It is interesting to examine some for illustrative purposes.

A solitary man who has a casual, non-resident, relationship with a much older woman answered simply: "A woman older than me . . . is good to have," "A woman younger than me . . . is very bad to have." A man with a woman just a little older than he: "A woman older than me . . . is good to keep," "A woman younger than me . . . is very nice to have fun with." In other words, the kind of woman he wants to establish permanent relations with is not someone he considers "fun." A man whose woman is a good deal older than he: "A woman older than me . . . she really older than me—she does treat me very good." A woman younger than me: "You take up a companion older [sic] than you, you will satisfy yourself. You know she older than you and you will stop there." This man will not even consider a younger woman. What he desires from a woman is seen in his response to the stem "Women." "Women . . . a woman is good to us because they keep us clean and get our little supper and will protect it [keep the supper warm]." There are many clues to this man's needs in his last remark. First, women are good because they take care of him. This dependency need is brought out in his choice of words to describe her ways with food—she "will protect it." There is also a further sense of self pity in his characterization of the food as "little supper." A last example is the case of a young man who has a woman several years older. "A woman older than me . . . they want to rule me with what I have, and don't want me to rule them at all with their own things." He is reacting somewhat against the domination of the older woman, but still prefers her to the young girls, for as he says, "A woman younger than me . . . I like to keep myself from them. Because sometime their mouth is really tougher than mine, and mine is real easy. So, I like to keep myself from them." Throughout his protocol this man constantly avoids any interpersonal confrontation, preferring always to be alone and avoid trouble and troublemakers. He consistently sees other people as leading him astray or trying to harm him.

On the other hand, many of the men with younger women demonstrate that while they should respect an older woman—probably because they have their mother in mind—a younger woman is someone to be nurtured. For example, here are the replies of two men with younger women with whom they have had large families: 1) "A woman older than me . . . should be able to give me some instruction in the world." "A woman younger than me . . . I should show her something. I should teach her something." 2) "A woman older than me . . . must show them some kind of respect." "A woman younger than me . . . you have to take good care of her." Neither of these men demands care from the older woman. They both feel free to pay her the homage due her position or to benefit from the advice of her experience, without developing this image of an older woman into one of maternal support. Similarly, they both welcome a younger woman as a chance to express their own capacities for nurturing and support.

The different psychological attitudes toward women come out most clearly on the stems "A wife," and "Women," which were used in hopes of evaluating the quality of the male-female relationships. The responses clustered in the following categories:

1. affirmative, personal comments, e.g., "is loving and kind," "is pleasant to have," and "is a good company";
2. statements that the woman takes care of the man, e.g., "keeps you clean," "to take care of me," and "is really useful";
3. negative comments, e.g., "some are very peculiar," "sometimes a woman is a little disagreeable."

The comparisons of the two groups are found in Tables 9-8 and 9-9.

TABLE 9-8

Responses to the sentence completion stem: "A Wife"

	I. Affirmative	II. Woman Takes Care	III. Negative	IV. Does Not Have
Fishermen	12	0	1	2
Cane Cutters	6	5	1	4

I vs. II, < .025 (Fisher test)

From this material one feels the psychological forces that lead to the choice of an older or younger woman. It seems clear that those who choose an older woman desire to be protected, cleansed, and fed, as children are, and to be treated as they were not when they were children. They are not deeply interested in the satisfactions of personal contacts. Those who choose younger

TABLE 9-9

Responses to the sentence completion stem: "Women"

	I. Affirmative	II. Woman Takes Care	III. Negative
Fishermen	7	3	4
Cane Cutters	2	9	3

I vs. II, $p < .025$ (Fisher test)
I vs. II + III, $p < .05$

women, on the other hand, have much more of a need for affectionate relationships, as well as a desire to be the ones who provide the care and nurturing for their mates.

Several conclusions may be drawn from the fact that cane cutters tend to mate with older women and fishermen with younger women. First, this supports my contention that legal marriage in this village is an institution geared to the gratification of the need for security. Older women seem to be seen as more trained and capable, better able to take care of the man as well as emotionally undemanding. Second, in structural terms, it may be taken as a principle of recruitment for the family. Although relative age positions are clearly demographic facts, they also establish a psychological continuum. Mates are then selected on the basis of their place on this dimension. If we are to understand why a particular mate with certain demographic characteristics is chosen, it is essential to evaluate the meaning of these facts for the act of choosing. Third, the reasons behind the difference in the mates' relative age introduces a topic which will be dealt with in detail in Section II of this chapter. Just as the cane-cutting gang and the fishing crew are based on different principles, so their family groups are differently organized. In the choice of the relative age of their mate, cane cutters seem to be structuring the male-female relationship into an institution which satisfies their need for security in much the same manner as the economic activity they choose.

Fishermen, not functioning on this level, have been freed to organize the activities of their family group around a higher need—the need for love. In the next section it will become clear how these general principles come to dominate the entire structure of the family.

Before concluding, one possible objection must be considered. It might be argued that because so many of the cane cutters are from other islands they are less desirable to the women of Dieppe Bay, and the only women they can attract are the older "used-up" ones least appealing to the men of the village.

This objection may be met by a close study of the age and birthplace characteristics of the female population. First, of the eleven men who mate with older women, six were born on the island and five were born off the island. If the alternative explanation were correct there would be a strong imbalance in favor of the off-island men. However, this ratio of native and foreign born is approximately the same as that found in the total sample. Second, if we assume that women 33 years old or younger constitute that group which is the most attractive and least "used-up," it is most reasonable to expect that they should have the least difficulty in finding mates, and, therefore, should be mated with men older than themselves. The reasoning here is that for this age group, men older than they would be steadier workers and better providers than younger men. The fact is that of the six women in this age group, three live with older men and three with younger. If we analyze the entire sample of women the same ratio is found. Women residing with younger men are spread evenly through the whole population.

II. THE STRUCTURE OF THE FAMILY

The Negro family in the West Indies has entered the literature of social science as a prime example of the distortions created by life on the fringe of industrial society. Minimal income, uncertain economic conditions, low status in the total society, and racial prejudice are frequently cited to explain the marginality of the male within his family group. The family is seen as primarily composed of a relationship between the mother and her children, with the father, at best, peripheral and uninvolved. His role is mainly that of the economic provider, and in return he gets his meals, clean clothes, a clean house and sexual privileges. When the mother-child relationship is expanded to include others, the link is seen as extending through the female to her sisters or to her mother (the grandmother household). In the words of a prominent student of the West Indian family, Raymond Smith, the man . . .

> although de jure head of the household group (if present) is usually marginal to the complex of internal relationships of the group. By marginal we mean that he associates infrequently with the other members of the group and is on the fringe of the effective ties which bind the group together (Smith, 1960).

1. Relations Between the Man and his Children

Establishing the structure of relationships is one of the most basic tasks required in the analysis of the family, and, in many ways, is the most difficult. In order to obtain systematic data on this problem in Dieppe Bay two questions were included in the Female Interview: "What is a father supposed to do for the children?" and "What is a mother supposed to do for the children?" The replies uncovered two very dissimilar types of family arrangements organized on the bases discussed earlier in this chapter and in the previous chapters on economic activities. The answers to the two questions of the Female Interview may be summarized as follows. The cane cutter's family structure appears to be similar to that model found in the literature on the Negro family in which the father is marginal to the dominant mother-child relationship. Further, it will be seen in Section III that inclusion of additional members in the family—such as a sister or mother—exclusively follows the female line. The family of the fishermen, on the other hand, is an integrated unit in which the father is extremely active and assumes responsibility for many tasks in regard to the children which the cane cutter leaves to the mother. Also, it will be seen below that the male and female themselves interact over a much greater range of activities than is the case in cane cutter's families.

These men are products of the same sociological groups —as measured by the economic activities of their parents, subject to the same intensity of economic dislocation— have roughly the same number of months with low income, enjoy approximately the same degree of economic benefit from their labor, possess the same range of skin color, and together share the same low status in the total society. Yet the internal structure of the family, in terms of the marginality of the males, is extremely different. Therefore, since there is this difference, the peripheral nature of the male in his family is clearly not simply due to the factor of working on "the fringe of Western industrial society." By comparing these two groups of men, who possess such strikingly different family arrangements, we can begin to discover those specific determinants that produce the effect of male marginality.

The methodological differences between this study and most others in this field must be understood. It is the usual practice for the investigator to make a census of the entire village and base his conclusions on the data presented by all the occupations within that village or the data from all the varieties and intensities of employment within one occupation. This was not my aim, and so data are not available on the broken families, higher-status families, families of estate workers at jobs other than cutting, or the casual, transient, emigrant, or ineffectual worker's family. The men whom I have studied are those lower-class laborers most committed and most successful—within, of course, the range of possibilities permitted by the conditions of their employment. In this way, I can present a more "pure" case for the study of the determinants of family structure and the data are unobscured by these extraneous phenomena.

The responsibilities of the mother for her children are presented in Table 9-10. In both groups the mother has similar responsibilities. She must feed and clean the children, send them to school and to church, teach them manners, and look after their well-being in many ways.

However, the duties of the father are quite different in the two groups. See Table 9-11. In both, his primary job

Table 9-10

Responsibility of mother for children

Responsibilities	The number of responses fishermen's women give in each category	The number of responses cane cutters' women give in each category
1. Look after them in all ways	3	—
2. Care them	3	4
3. Food	7	11
4. Clean clothes	6	10
5. Protect them	1	—
6. Send to school regularly	9	7
7. Bathe skin	6	10
8. Food on time	1	—
9. Church	3	6
10. Sunday school	2	3
11. Keep the house tidy for them	1	—
12. Carry them to doctor	2	5
13. Help secure job when grown	1	—
14. Obedience	1	1
15. Respect	1	—
16. Give licks	—	1
17. Put to sleep for nap	1	2
18. Nurse them	1	—
19. Give them a walk	1	—
20. Bring them up in fear of God	1	1
21. Keep them from bad company	1	2
22. Buy them books and school supplies	2	1
23. Buy them medicine	1	—
24. Buy them clothes	3	3
25. Teach to walk polite in road	1	3
26. Teach them manners	1	2
27. Teach them right from wrong	1	2
28. Belch them	1	—

TABLE 9-10 (*Continued*)

29. Work for them	—	1
30. School them so they will help mother when big	—	1
31. Give them good promotion if you can afford it	—	1
32. Have them help her work in ground	—	1
33. Ask Lord for help in raising	—	1
Total responses	61	80
	N = 11	N = 13

is to support the family—virtually every woman mentions this fact. But the cane cutter is clearly a marginal figure in the life of the child. His most important task, beyond support, is to discipline the child and teach him manners. Items such as "proper behavior," "teach them not to do wrong," "give them licks," and "rule the children," are heavily stressed. None of the duties most frequently mentioned involve much personal contact with the child and seldom reflect nurturing attitudes or prescribe tasks demanding a degree of empathy. The children are very much the responsibility of the mother, and the male is useful only in providing the financial resources and the strong right arm. It may be said that his relationship with his child is most superficial and his personal intervention is solely geared to produce a child who will not embarrass him in the community.

Just as the fisherman is concerned with establishing a crew in which he is interdependent and interactive with the other members, so too does he demand the same with his family. He is responsible for the support of his family—obviously a prerequisite for its maintenance. Yet his obligations and concerns go much deeper. It is important to notice in Table 9-11 that, in contradistinction to the cane cutters, he does not function as a moralist. Very few responses are of the category, "proper behavior." Rather, his role seems to be much more nurturant, thoroughly implicating him in the care and fostering of his

Table 9-11

Responsibility of father for children

Responsibilities	The number of responses fishermen's women give in each category	The number of responses cane cutters' women give in each category
1. Support them	8	10
2. Teach them not to do wrong	1	4
3. Proper behavior	1	6
4. Prevent them from getting in trouble—going astray	2	—
5. See they obey parents	1	—
6. See they obey the mother	1	1
7. Responsibility is same as mother	2	—
8. Handle people's complaints of kids	2	—
9. Stand up for them if people beat them	—	1
10. Give them licks	—	1
11. Treat them good	2	—
12. Help care and raise them	3	—
13. Help the mother	1	—
14. School	—	1
15. Church	—	1
16. Care in mother's absence	—	2
17. Love them	1	1
18. Bury a dead child	—	1
19. Scold if they do wrong	—	1
20. Help out if they are sick and mother can't take them to doctor	—	1
21. Carry to work in his grounds	—	1
22. Set them a model by not drinking	—	1
23. Supervise them	1	—

Table 9-11 *(Continued)*

24. Rule the children	—	2
25. Make them not be rude to people	—	1
Total responses	26	36
	N = 11	N = 13

children. He is to "help the mother" with the children, his "responsibility is the same as the mothers," and he is to "help care and raise them." Another task is to "treat them good"; he is to indulge the child and bring him presents. In other words, the fisherman is active in the functioning of the family and shares with the mother many of the daily tasks.

This is not to say that there is no sexual division of labor. The woman is much more responsible than the man for the care of the children, which is her main job, even when she is working full-time on the estates. But if the fisherman does help in the care of the children, assumes some of the responsibility for their education and guidance, plays with and indulges them, we may then safely conclude that he is a meaningful figure in their lives. And the reverse must also be true—his children are among the most significant people in his own universe.

Another indication of the father's concern for his children is the quality of the supervision and authority he exerts over them. For the cane cutter the issue is one of teaching the children manners. The fisherman, rather, is concerned with the sort of person his child will become and his discipline is designed to protect the child. Therefore, his obligations are to "prevent them from getting into trouble," and to "prevent them from going astray." When the child gets into trouble with other people the father is expected to intervene and smooth out the problem, although he will, of course, punish the child if he has done something wrong. The crucial difference is that the fisherman will not do so automatically, but tends to stop and consider the child as an individual before punishing him.

The replies to the question "What is a father supposed to do for the children?" were analyzed on this dimension—from superficial to involved personal relationships. Each task was scored separately, with the exception of the category of "support," which is equally present in both groups and is not related to this particular issue. The results of this analysis are given in Table 9-12.

Table 9-12

Quality of relationship between father and children

	Superficial	Involved
Fishermen	4	14
Cane Cutters	21	5

$$X^2 = 12.57$$
$$p < .001$$

Of all the large families in the village, the fishermen's families made a greater ceremony of working together, building additions onto their houses and tending their gardens. One of the families has gone so far as to put up the motto "In Unity there is Strength" in ten inch high letters on a trellis in its yard. The large cane cutters' families are much more fragmented. When I would visit I heard tales of the ingratitude of various members of the family, how difficult it was to get them to help or how much had been sacrificed to send one to England and how little return is expected from that "transaction."

2. Relations between the Man and Woman

When we examine the quality of the relationship between the man and woman, the same structural difference emerges. Just as the cane cutter was disengaged from his children, so too is he in his relationship with his woman. He does not share in many activities with her; never helps her with the cooking; seldom eats with her; and tends to claim he owns things separately from her. The replies to the question on the Female Interview, "What does S like best about you?" brought out many

interesting aspects of their relationship. The women of
the cane cutters feel desired on the following bases. First,
physiological gratifications: she cooks his food and keeps
him clean. Second, she does not disturb him: "keeps
herself quiet," "doesn't startle him when he is asleep."
Third, a series of impersonal qualities: she works hard,
does not look sloppy, and she does not belittle him in public. Fourth, several women deny knowledge of the man's
feelings toward them entirely: "I don't know his mind.
His mind is his own." In general, in this family there is a
lack of interaction between the man and woman with
little affection between them, or delight in each other's
company. Everything is seen as a quid pro quo—he gives
money and she gives physiological gratification.

The relationship between the fisherman and his woman
shows much more involvement in each other's life. The
man often helps the woman cook and usually eats together with her and their children. He also claims that
they own many things together. A fisherman will often
make the statement, with a grandiloquent sweep of his
arm, that everything he owns, house, chairs, boats, nets,
pots belongs to everyone in the family. He is also likely
to proclaim that everyone in the family works together
and helps care for each other's animals.

The women of the fishermen put more emphasis on
personal qualities and less stress on their physiological
attractions. They feel that the fishermen enjoy their
"company," and take pleasure in their ability to sit down
for a talk and give good advice. A feeling of much greater
trust and interpersonal enjoyment between the man and
the woman comes through their replies.

This difference in quality of the man-woman relationship may be further underscored if the conclusions drawn
from the discussion of relative age positions are recalled.
The desire of the cane cutters for older women, trained
in domestic affairs, is the product of their basic desire
for secure, unemotional attachments. The desire of the
fishermen for younger women reflects their desire to receive warm personal gratifications. Together, these wishes
explain the difference in family organization. The cane
cutter is pressing for satisfaction of his need for security
and if he receives his food and bed is not interested in

Table 9-13

What the man likes best about the woman

Preferences	Fishermen's Women	Cutters' Women
1. I don't know his mind	1	3
2. Cook his food	2	3
3. Not displeased with food	1	—
4. Keeps him clean	2	4
5. Keeps the home tidy-clean	2	—
6. Cares him when he's sick	1	1
7. Sex play	1	3
8. Combs his hair	—	1
9. Doesn't startle him when he asleep	—	1
10. She works hard	—	2
11. Likes her to keep herself quiet	—	1
12. Likes her not to keep company	2	3
13. If kids looking clean	1	1
14. He likes me	1	1
15. He sometimes regrets marrying me	—	1
16. He criticizes me a lot	—	1
17. She keeps herself well	—	1
18. Doesn't make him look bad	—	1
19. He likes to see a woman in his home	—	1
20. She is courteous	—	1
21. When she does right	—	1
22. She amuses him	—	1
23. Her ways	2	—
24. She doesn't quarrel (like other women)	1	—
25. Listens to what he says	2	—
26. Doesn't hide things from him	1	—
27. Her company	1	—
28. That she can sit down and talk	1	—
29. Sometimes compliments her cooking	1	—
30. If she gives him good advice	1	—
31. She tries to do everything to make him feel good	1	—
32. She is not wild	1	—
33. She is strict to his order	1	—

TABLE 9-13 (*Continued*)

34. She didn't stray about	1	—
35. She encouraged him to go to church	1	—
36. He is pleased with whatever she did to him	1	—
37. The way she does her work	1	~
Total responses	31	32
	N = 11	N = 15

searching for more. The fisherman, satisfied at this level, has much greater interest in interpersonal gratifications and establishes ties to many people. Therefore, his network of significant personages is much more developed than that of the cane cutter. The comparison of the two groups is presented in Tables 9-13 and 9-14.

TABLE 9-14

The quality of the relationship between the man and the woman

	Interactive	Non-Interactive
Fishermen	15	14
Cane Cutters	8	24
		$X^2 = 5.26$
		$p < .025$

If we ask the women why they, in turn, have established these different types of relationships, the data I have gathered are not as full as those available for the men. This is primarily due to the fact that I came to this question late in my field work and was unable to take similar personality measures. In hopes of partially answering these questions, or, at a minimum, establishing objectively the existence of certain states in the woman, I included several questions of a somewhat projective nature on the Female Interview.

One fact that sheds some light on why certain women

enter into, and others refuse to enter, involved personal relationships is that some women fear men and would prefer to live with their mothers. These women see men as selfish and dangerous—quick to anger and free with blows. To establish the existence of this attitude toward males, I asked the women on the Female Interview about the sex preference they have for children. The question read, "Would you rather have boy or girl babies." The assumption was that those women who feared men would state that they preferred girl babies, and would condemn boys as too much trouble, or reject them as bad by nature. The results are given in Table 9-15.

TABLE 9-15

Women's preference for children

	Woman Prefers		
	Girls	Boys	Both Boys and Girls
Fishermen's Women	2	3	6
Cane Cutters' Women	9	2	4

If we compare the categories "Girls" to a combined category of "Boys" and "Both" the results are clear. The reasoning in this case is that when a woman says that she likes both boys and girls, she is admitting an affection for a boy. Through this procedure we can isolate those women who insist they have no desire for a male at all. This is done in Table 9-16.

Fishermen's women seem to have no particular preference as to the sex of their children. They desire boys and girls equally and have no special fear or repugnance of either. Cane cutters' women have, on the other hand, a definite preference for girls. The language used tells us a good deal about the women's attitude toward males. One woman who likes boys says; "Boys. Girls are too much trouble. Boys too, but they're better; boys listen more to what you tell them than girls." A woman who likes both: "both, none more than the other. I love both.

TABLE 9-16

Women's preference for children

	Woman Prefers	
	Girls	Boys or Both
Fishermen's Women	2	9
Cane Cutters' Women	9	6

$p < .05$
(Fisher test)

Whatsoever come, girl or boy, it means the same." Those who prefer girls, however, are more emphatic. "I prefer girls, because boys sometimes bring you to shame." "I prefer to have one girl, boys too rude. You can control a girl good, once you mean to control it." And finally, "Girl babies. When boys grow up they give you trouble. Their deeds might kill you."

Although the women of the cane cutters have a definite preference for girls, it is interesting to note that each group of women has roughly the same percentage of boys and girls, so there is no question of either justifying what they have, or longing for what they do not have.

Another measure of the quality of male-female interaction is reflected in the degree to which the women acknowledge fighting with the man. In Chapter 5 I proposed that one of the most significant characteristics of the cane cutting gang was the extent to which the cutters were incapable of confronting each other. To recapitulate, the structure of the gang is that of men laboring in isolation from each other. When an injustice is done, the injured party does not feel the power to make an issue of it, and complainingly retreats into himself. This lack of personal power also has its effect on the positive mode of confrontation—the men are unable to cooperate with each other for a common end. The result is a structure with few rich bonds between the members. The fishing crew is, in many respects, a unit in which the men have little fear to challenge a wrong. If anything, there is a combative eagerness to force the issue. This is one of the roots of the crew structure which produces an interactive organization with many ties between the members. In the projective test, this difference in psychological state of each group was clearly demonstrated.

This difference similarly occurs within the family. In the cane cutter's family there is a denial of aggression as a means of interpersonal contact. The women talk at great lengths of the wrongs done to them; complaining that the man beats them, drinks too much, or runs around with women. Most of the women, while feeling the injury, seem not to wish to quarrel about it, and minimize whatever fighting occurs, or has occurred. Probably this does not reflect the exact state of affairs, for I know of quarrels among those couples who deny any sort of violence. It does portray correctly, I believe, the psychological relationship between the man and the woman and indicates a relative poverty in the affective ties between the woman and the man.

The women of the fishermen have the same number of complaints about their men but, as they are not defending themselves against emotional reactions, seem to have no fear of creating an incident. In this way the fisherman's family is similar in structure to his economic unit. In both there exist many bonds and channels of contact which are not established in the life of the cane cutter.

Here are some examples of the ways the women express themselves on this subject. First, those women who answer that they do fight with the man.

> "Oh, a lot. About the children. If we disagree about what the children are doing, where they are going. Sometimes if I want to go somewheres he starts quarreling, but he feels he can go where he likes."

> "Sometimes. All we curse, yes. Tongue and teeth must knock. According if I don't do things to suit him, or if he don't do things to suit me."

> "Many times, bad fights. And at night, if I ain't feeling good and deprive him. If I beat the girl who is his favorite."

Second, those who are trying to suppress the idea of quarreling.

> "Yes, used to, not now. Once he broke my arm. Used to fight when he was drinking . . . Used to have words about his drinking."

"Used to have talking quarreling [i.e., not hitting]. If he's drunk he'll make talk about anything at all."

Third, those who deny this completely.

"Not at all. Not since I'm here."
"He won't obey. He drinks rum with his friends and when I correct him he says it's his money, or if I doesn't like it I can leave the home. This brings contention. I leave it to the Lord."

The responses are categorized in Table 9-17. In Table

TABLE 9-17

Aggression between men and women

	Forms of Aggression		
	Fights	Used to Fight	Never Fights
Fishermen's Women	8	1	2
Cane Cutter's Women	4	8	2

9-18 I have combined the replies stating that the woman never fights with those claiming she has renounced fighting, because these two categories have in common the

TABLE 9-18

Aggression between men and women

	Interpersonal Aggression	Denial of Inter- personal Aggression
Fishermen's Women	8	3
Cane Cutter's Women	4	10

$p < .05$
(Fisher test)

denial of interpersonal aggression as a mode of relationship. When contrasted to those who proclaim its use we are able to get another measure of degree of personal intimacy and ease in relating. This brings us to the theme of this section. When two people feel free to quarrel with each other, we have an indication that they do respond to each other and that ties exist between them. When there is a fear of quarreling as an avenue of relation, we may conclude that the affective depth of the links are diminished.

One last indication of the cane cutters' lack of involvement with their families may be found in the replies the women gave in their evaluation of men. The question was "What would you say are the worst things about men?" Some of the complaints were similar to those just presented. The man drinks too much, or runs after women, or else beats her. There was, however, one new problem brought out in these answers. Almost half (7 of 15) of the cane cutters' women complained that the man does not give them enough money to support the home. Only one out of twelve fishermen's women brought up this issue. In relative terms this indicates that the fisherman is seen by the woman as much more committed to his family. Once again, the psychological implications of this fact are more important than the economic realities. Since the cane cutters' women say they spend more money in the shops than the fishermen's women (the fishermen average $10.33 per week in the shop, and the cane cutters $12.52 per week), they are, in fact, getting more money from their men. The psychological implication of non-support goes beyond the literal truth of providing money, and conveys a sense of general non-support of the family by the cane cutter. The data on female complaints are presented below, Table 9-19.

TABLE 9-19

Women's complaints about their men

	Non-Support	Other Complaints
Fishermen's Women	1	11
Cane Cutters' Women	7	8

$p < .05$
(Fisher test)

In this regard, it is interesting to examine the responses of the men to the Sentence Completion stem, "A family." The cane cutters do not show a dominant nurturing attitude. Primarily they reflect a concern with the necessity of providing for their family and frequently indicate that this was a strain. One man responded ". . . is one of my worries. [They] may go astray because I don't have money to support." The fishermen do not carry this burden, for none mention the question of support at all! Instead, they demonstrate a feeling of nurturance— A family . . . "not just children. Whole relative between mother and father," or else a casual acceptance of the family—"is nice to have"—without great emphasis in either direction. See Table 9-20.

TABLE 9-20

Men's attitude toward their family

	I Problem with Support	II Positive Attitude	III Negative Attitude
Fishermen	0	10	3
Cane Cutters	6	8	2

$p < .025$
(Fisher test)
I vs. II

These together, the men's responses on the Sentence Completion Test and the women's on the Female Interview, portray a state in which the family is a difficult burden for the cane cutter. If the women feel that the men do not support the family, this reflects a general and profound lack of trust in the supportive abilities of the male and leads to the conclusion that the ties between the man and woman in the cane cutter's family are much more tenuous and shallow than in the fisherman's.

3. Relations between the Family and the Village

Thus far we have discussed the ties between the men and their women and children. I would like to turn now from the internal processes of the family to an examination of the mode of relationship between the individuals of each group and the rest of the community.

The same ability of the fishermen to maintain relatively rich personal associations with their women and children impels them to form many relationships with other members of the community. They find much pleasure in these contacts and through them set up a fairly wide network of friendly relationships, which they integrate with those they have established in their own family. Although their family is a relatively warm place, it is not a refuge from the rest of the community, and the enjoyment they find in the company of others in the street is brought into the home. There is a fair amount of visiting (talking and drinking) which takes place in the house and provides for the fishermen an all-inclusive life space of relationships within the whole village.

The dominant fact of the cane cutter's world is that they are afraid to let people in. Although their family is not warm, it is still a refuge from the strains of daily life. The men socialize in the rum shops or on the street, but insist on a definite separation between the street and their homes. Their family is a haven and forms an encapsulated group shut off from the rest of the community's activities.

The meaning and purpose of the two types of families may be seen with remarkable vividness in the physical setting of their houses. As the observer approaches them he is struck by what is truly a proclamation of the difference in intent of the inhabitants. Surrounding most of the houses of the cane cutters is a high, expensive, and often, impenetrable fence. Sometimes made of board and discarded sheets of metal, other times of tightly packed and carefully tended tall bushes, the fence serves, as is consciously recognized, to keep people away. The houses of the fishermen, on the other hand, are usually set out in an open piece of land, without any fence at all, inviting free access to the house and giving ease in passing on to those of its neighbors.

I was first impressed with the meaning of the fence in Dieppe Bay at a time when I was very puzzled at what seemed to me to be an extraordinary emphasis on privacy and secrecy among some of my friends. For example, when we returned to the village for the second time, I wrote ahead and some friends set up a house for us. We were given a screen to divide one room in two and provide a hiding place for eating. When we complained that the screen took up too much room and suggested that perhaps someone else might have a use for it, the owner moved it into the bedroom so that we could hide behind it when dressing. When I pointed out that the shutters on the window could easily be closed so no one could look in, she hung a curtain across a corner and suggested that we could dress behind that. All in all, it took a week and a half to get the screen out of the house. Another time, this woman invited us to store our trunks in an unused house she was building for her son down the street. But the moving had to be done at night. When I asked why, she and another woman said at one time, "what you cannot see you cannot tell." Then her friend explained, dramatically, "They would say; Man! Mr. Aronoff gave Mrs. P. a B-I-G trunk."

As I was trying to understand what was so frightening in what other people might say, and why they were so vulnerable, I had a talk with the sergeant of police who was stationed in the village. He claimed that a fence was put up for two reasons. First, to keep animals in the yard and prevent them from being stolen. Second, to keep out trespassers. He felt that a fence gives privacy and insures that no one will overhear your conversations; "People find a lot of time to talk someone else's business." I asked him for an example and he gave this one. "Mrs. accuses Mr. of going out with Jane. A person going through the yard could overhear and tell Jane. Jane comes back and accuses Mrs. of scandalizing her name. Jane could take her to court, if the eavesdropper will go too."

This need for secrecy in putting up fences seems, to me, to be a valuable indication of the manner in which these people relate to others. There are so often instances, which would usually appear as somewhat paranoid if they were not so often rooted in the actual fact, in which the villagers exhibit great fears of the hostility of their neighbors. The fences appear, then, to express mistrust of those about them, and serve as evidence of the extent to which they cut themselves off from one another. Since these people are themselves so often cruel to others, it does not take us too far from the data to speculate that this fear has a reciprocal basis, and that what is often feared is the retaliation for those hostile wishes of their own. This is clear in the police sergeant's story. Mr. and Mrs. have a fence so that Jane will not be able to retaliate for the wrongs done to her.

A fence, then, tells us much about the nature of the family. On the one hand it is a specific piece of material culture whose presence or absence is completely dependent upon the psychological state of the individuals. On the other, it enables us to evaluate quickly and easily the relationship between the family and the rest of the community. The results of scoring the enclosed nature of the family area are presented in Table 9-21. Although

TABLE 9-21

Distribution of fences and occupation

	Fence	No Fence
Fishermen	5	10
Cane Cutters	12	5
		$x^2 = 3.07$
		$p < .05$

most of the areas were definitely either open or thoroughly closed, a small number, three in each group, were difficult to score; because they were either houses built next to one or two ruined stone walls—therefore, partly set off, but not deliberately; or they had a few low shrubs bordering the property—defining the boundary, but permitting access. These I called semi-fenced and scored separately. Because they were so difficult to interpret, and for the sake of making a comparison of those groups which definitely do or do not have fences, they were dropped from the test.

The police sergeant suggested a possible alternative interpretation, which must be carefully considered because it is much simpler than the psychological explanation. He felt that people put up fences to protect their property and livestock. Indeed, he felt this was the dominant motive for the act. If we consider the association of property and livestock with the existence of fences it becomes evident that this alternative possibility must be ruled out. The first evidence we have is that fishermen leave wire mesh, wooden poles and finished traps around their houses, while the cutters have no such equipment in their yards. Yet it is the cutters and not the fishermen who have fences. Second, if true, it would be expected that there would be a strong correlation between ownership of livestock and fences. Fishermen have more chickens and pigs than cutters and still have many fewer fences. There is also no correlation between the number of animals and fences—contrary to the prediction of this alternative explanation. We may notice in Table 9-22

TABLE 9-22

Distribution of fences by occupation for men who have pigs

	Distribution of Fences	
	Fence	No Fence
Fishermen	2	6
Cane Cutters	3	4

that 3 of the 5 fences the fishermen have are possessed by men who do not have any pigs (the pig is the main animal kept in the yard), and 8 of the 11 cutters who have fences do not have any pigs. Similarly, of the 7 people who own 10 or more chickens, only 2 have built a fence around their house. This alternative hypothesis, although reasonable, is not in accord with the real situation.

The same finding also emerges from the female protocols. The fisherman's woman is often visited in the home as she goes about her round of domestic activities. Her friends drop in when they choose, occasionally help her in her work and stay to chat about the happenings of the day, when the work is done. Significantly, the fisherman does not prohibit her from having her friends in, which is the case with many other village families.

When questioned, the cane cutters' women reveal great mistrust of the motives of others. They often claim that they have few friends and usually say that they never let anyone into their house, because a visitor is only seeking news with which to hurt them. The housework is done first, alone, and then if they have spare time, they leave their yard and go out into the street to talk or visit friends.

In order to establish these different modes of relating to the community in objective form for the whole sample, I asked the following question on the Female Interview: "When you are doing your home domestic work, do friends sometimes help you or keep you company or talk to you while you do the work?" Responses were scored in two categories: those who share the world inside the house with friends in some way, and those who shut their homes off from visitors. The results for the two groups are given in Table 9-23.

TABLE 9-23

Relationship of home to community

| | Relation of Home to Community | |
	Integrated into Community	Separated from Community
Fishermen's Women	9	4
Cane Cutters' Women	2	13

$p < .005$
(Fisher test)

A feeling for the different attitudes may be gained from the words they use to declare their positions. First, several examples from fishermen's women.

"Yes. A friend will come and help wash and iron and then sit down [to] chat and so."

"Friends generally come to talk, but not to help." (Do you enjoy talking with them?) "Yes."

"When friends come work is all done. I like when they come after work."

". . . If I'm washing and someone comes to ask a question I continue working with them . . . Sometimes friends keep you back. I like if they talk and help."

Some responses of cane cutters' women:

"No! Don't like friends. Sometimes friends bring contention. Bring too much news. Tell your business outside."

"Oh no! Myself alone and children. Don't love too much company!" (Why?) "They don't be true and most deceiving. Best to keep by yourself."

"No, don't keep friends. They only come to see what you have and when they're done they abuse you about it."

"I . . . make hello's in the street, not home. People want to know your business too much around here."

"No, no no! I don't keep friends. When you think you have a friend and talk, they turn it over again. I don't keep friends."

With these words the women summarize for us the different nature of the cane cutters' and the fishermen's families. The cane cutters' attitude is that visitors want to make trouble in the home and find out secrets to spread throughout the village. So they are mistrustful and suspicious of other people's motives. For protection they shut themselves off from the larger village community and form isolated encapsulated units.

Summary. The basic principles which organize the cane cutters' family life are the need for security, the need to be taken care of and the incapacity to become deeply involved in the lives of other people—whether wife, children, or friends. Their childhood experiences have left them hostile to the world and fearful of the consequences of establishing personal attachments. This avoidance is clearly evident in the fence they use to ward off the rest of the community.

The poverty of emotional relationships between the male and the rest of the family, so often described in the literature as the Negro-family type in the West Indies, that results in the male's marginal state in the family is due, I believe, to the specific conditions of his childhood, as discussed in Chapter 4, which fixate him on the safety level of personality. He is not able to constitute his family on any other basis.

The fisherman's family is, relatively speaking, a much more thoroughly integrated structure. His family is not shut off from the rest of the community; instead, there are many links which bind his household with village life. He is much more able to relate to other people and establish a family in which he is a significant figure. The relative security he enjoyed as a child and the greater gratification of his love needs have allowed him to progress to higher levels of personality, and so has permitted him to expand and develop his network of significant inter-personal relationships. The fisherman's childhood, in the same socio-economic environment as the cane cutter, as well as his early labor on the estates, demonstrates that the usual marginality of the male in the Negro family is neither a reflex of, nor necessary to, the plantation economy.

III. HOUSEHOLD COMPOSITION

The usual procedure of the anthropologist studying West Indian family life is to enter a community and, after a period of reciprocal familiarization, proceed with a survey of household forms. Because the family is such an ever-changing phenomenon, in which the participants may be present one month and gone the next, eating in one house and sleeping in another, contributing support to many people geographically dispersed, as well as frequently claiming equal allegiance to separate groups of people, the observer looking for a family often has the impression of peering through a kaleidoscope that operates according to no determined set of rules. Faced with these problems, the anthropologist seeking some element of order so that he may, at least, begin, decides that the house, itself, offers some measure of stability and, therefore, makes that his primary object of study.

His question is simply: who are the members of the household (therefore implying the family) and what are the principles determining its composition? Because the household reflects at least some aspects of family life, and because it has been the focus of the greatest part of the research on the family in the Caribbean, the first section of the Male Interview was devoted to a number of questions dealing with the forms household composition takes in the sample.

Given that the history, economic marginality, low status and ethnicity of the two groups of men are similar (the variables frequently used to explain differences in household composition), little difference would be predicted in the form the household would take in Dieppe Bay. Yet, upon completion of the interviewing, the forms of household composition were found to be dissimilar in crucial respects.

The fishermen live in four types of households: the man alone; the man and his woman; the man, woman, and their children; and the man, woman, their children and a grandchild who was born to one of their children (the grandchild's parents are absent). The common element in all these households is that every person, other than the man and woman, is related to every other on both sides.

The cane cutters have the first three forms the fishermen possess, but the predominant number are of a more complex nature. There are the following types of households: the man and his woman and her mother; the man and woman and children she had by another man; several variations of this last category, in which there are children of both the man and the woman as well as those related only to her, or her mother, or her sister's child, or her grandchildren born to one of her children by another man. In contradistinction to the fishermen, who are related to everyone in the household by blood, the common element in the cane cutters' household is that he is often related to members only through his connections to the woman. In the case of the fishermen we have an instance of the simple nuclear family. In the case of the cane cutters we have a variety of complex matrilateral families (i.e., kin related through ties to the female). In Table 9-24 are listed

Table 9-24

Household composition

Membership	Occupation	
	Fishermen	Cane Cutters
1. Man, woman and their children.	9	4
2. Man alone.	6	4
3. Man, woman, their children and her children.	—	3
4. Man and woman.	2	1
5. Man, woman, their children and their grandchildren.	2	—
6. Man, woman, woman's mother and grandchildren.	—	1
7. Man, woman and adopted child. (woman's sister's child)	—	1
8. Man, woman, their children, her children and her cousin.	—	1
9. Man, woman and her grandchild.	—	1
10. Man, woman, their children, her children, her mother, and her sister's child.	—	1
11. Man, woman, their children and her grandchildren.	—	1
12. Man, woman and her children.	—	1
13. Man, woman and her child-in-law.	—	1
14. Man, mother-in-law and her present mate.	—	1

the households found in this sample in Dieppe Bay, and the frequency of each case. Table 9-25 summarizes the households according to each of the dimensions.

Why should such a difference in household composition exist in groups that are so similar sociologically? To solve this problem we must determine why there are so many children included in the cane cutter's household who are not related to the man. The first fact of interest is the number of children born to the man and woman in each group. Since the fishermen are an older group and so would be expected to have more children, for com-

Table 9-25

Types of household and occupation

	Household			
	I Nuclear Family	II Complex Family	III Man and Woman	IV Solitary Man
Fishermen	11	0	2	6
Cane Cutters	4	12	1	4

I vs. II, $X^2 = 11.96$, p $<$ .001

parative purposes it is necessary to standardize the ages of the men. Of the men who range from 30 to 48 years of age (7 fishermen and 9 cutters) the fishermen have an average of 5.57 children in their household and the cutters 5.22 children. However, with their present mates the cutters' women have an average of only 3.55 children, as compared with the above-mentioned 5.52 for the fishermen's women. Therefore, although there are equal numbers of children in each household, the cutters' women had many more of these children with other men.

When we examine the duration of the union, for the standard age groups, we note that the fishermen have been living with their women for much greater periods of time. The fishermen have lived with the women for an average of seventeen years and the cane cutters for an average of eleven years. Since the age of the women is the same for the two groups we may conclude that the fishermen were with their women through most of their childbearing period, whereas the cane cutters were not.

This opens up two further questions. Were the women of the cutters living with other men during the period prior to this relationship, and, were they bearing children for other men during this time? Few women in either group have ever lived with another man: three of thirteen for the fishermen's women and two of fifteen for the cane cutters' women. At the same time, the women in both groups were bearing children for other men. Eight of the thirteen fishermen's women had a child by another man before the present relationship, as did twelve of fifteen cutters' women.

However, the cutters' women had many more children by previous relationships than did the fishermen's.[5] Their median number of children previous to the present spouse is 2.5, while the median of the fishermen's women is 0.5. For the matched group the medians are 2 and 0, respectively. What is more, the cutters' women have had these children with many more men. In eight of fifteen cases the cutters' women had children with two or more men, while this is true for only two of twelve fishermen's women.

This brings us to two conclusions. Because the length of the fisherman's union averages seventeen years, those few children born prior to the mating are, at present, too old to be included in the parental household. Therefore, no pool of "outside" children exists which might be expected to be residing with their mothers.

The cane cutters' women present a different life pattern. They have spent a large part of their child-bearing years outside their present union. During this time they have had many children, often by many men. When they came to form their permanent union they already were the mothers of a large number of children. It must be remembered that although they had children by many other men they never resided with them. This is usually the first conjugal residence unit they have entered. Since the women average eleven years with their present mates, the children they had previously are often young, and so, contrary to the situation among the fishermen, there are many young children to be taken care of; and it is these which are brought into the cane cutters' household.

Household membership, therefore, is not a "direct" function of a psychological need. The choice of the two types of household composition may be seen simply as a phenomenon based on the presence or absence of

[5] Several men admit to having fathered children with other women. All of these children remained with their mothers, who live in different villages.

young children fathered by other men before the establishment of this present union. When there are "outside"
children they are included in the household. There
are no grounds for assuming any special disinclination on
the part of the fishermen to bringing "outside" children
into their present family.

But is the matter disposed of so easily? Why has
one group of men taken in their women early, and the
other group waited a rather long period? Why have the
cane cutters not formed their unions at the beginning of
the child-bearing period of the women, as did the fishermen? [6] These are the crucial problems. An analysis of
these questions is required to complete our understanding of the forces creating the patterns of household composition.

As I have indicated, I do not feel that the variation
in household composition is produced by direct pressure
for the gratification of psychological needs. This has been
the case in the family structures previously discussed, but
it is not now the principle in operation. The determinants
of household composition, I believe, are an instance of
the indirect influence of psychological needs. This
concept has been discussed in Chapter 2. Briefly, a
psychological need can have an indirect influence on
the formation of a social unit if the direct gratification
of the need creates sociological states which then lead to
the formation of the unit under study.

Therefore, we must understand the reasons for the
presence of "outside" children with the cane cutters,
and their absence with the fishermen. What force could
be operating to produce this situation? Throughout this
chapter, and, indeed, the entire work, the two groups
of men have been seen to be striving for the gratification
of different needs. It is this differential in purpose which
is, again, at the heart of the matter.

Since the cane cutters are seeking "safety" gratifications, while the fishermen are seeking "love," the answer
to this problem is found in the qualities of the women

[6] For the matched group, the median age of the fishermen's
women's first union was 20 years, and the cane cutters' women's
first union was 29 years. In the sample, as a whole, the medians
are 21.5 and 27.5, respectively.

TABLE 9-26

Years with mother for the woman

				C															
C	F	F	C	C	C	F	F	F	C	F	C	C	C	C	C				
C	C	F	F	C	C	C	F	F	F	C	C	F	C	F	C	C	C	C	
3	6	9	13	14	15	16	18	19	20	21	22	23	24	27	29	30	32	33	56

Years with mother

C = cane cutters' women   F = fishermen's women

they choose. The question is now, what sort of woman will satisfy a need for safety, as opposed to a need for love? The problem may be resolved by examining Table 9-26.

Here we see that the two groups of men mate with women who have had very different kinds of childhood experiences. The fishermen mate with girls who leave home with the coming of biological and psychological adulthood. They left home primarily during the ages of 18 to 24. The cane cutters find women in one of two positions. The women have either lost their mothers in their childhood—from the age of three to sixteen, or else they have stayed on with their own mothers until quite late—from the age of 27 to 56. Few of their women left their mothers during the ages of 18-24. See Table 9-27.

TABLE 9-27

Years with mother for the woman

	Years with Mother	
	18-24	0-17, 25+
Fishermen's Women	7	5
Cane Cutters' Women	3	12
		p < .05
		(Fisher test)

What are the psychological consequences of this differential in childhood experience? Those women who lost their mothers early got a forced education in "taking care." They have had to learn to care for themselves and for their brothers and sisters, and so became a relatively experienced group in household matters. Further, as discussed previously (see Chapter 4), early loss produces a state of isolation and a diminishing of the capacity to form interpersonal relationships. As a result, these women would have sexual contact with men,[7] which

[7] In return for sexual favors, women expect to receive presents and small sums of money to supplement their income.

led in due course to having children (physiological gratifications), but they were afraid to establish more permanent relations. Only the burden of many children, more than they could manage themselves, forced them into their present permanent union.

The third group of women are products of a similar process. As they continued living with their mothers into their thirties, they had casual relations with men which resulted, often, in many children. As the number of their children increased, and as their mothers aged, an increasing burden of the household responsibilities devolved upon them. One would want to know why these women did not establish households with men while they were in their early twenties. Unfortunately, I have no information on this score, and it will have to be left as an unanswered, but critical question. What is clear is that the extensive training they did get as they assumed charge of their maternal household equipped them with capacities similar to the first group. Both result in a woman experienced in domestic matters and fully equipped to take charge and give care to a man, when she choses to mate.

The women who lived with their mothers until their early twenties were relatively free from this early harassment and domesticity.[8] They are a much more secure and responsive group of women, which may be clearly seen in some of the answers they gave to the more projective questions on the Female Interview (i.e., their responses to sex preferences of children, degree of friendship possessed and desired, etc.). They can more easily satisfy a man's need for affection. At the same time,

[8] An indication of the quality of their parental household may be seen in the number of years they completed in school. The Kittitian rural primary school system has seven grades. In order to complete the program, a child's family must encourage her to succeed (thereby demonstrating a concern for the child), and evidence both an economic ability to do without the money she might bring in and a good deal of her assistance in the purely domestic affairs of the household such as caring for younger children. The median grade the fishermen's women completed in school was 6, and the cane cutters' women, 4. This is significantly different at the .025 level, with the Fisher test. Furthermore, five fishermen's women completed the entire school program, whereas no cutters' women did.

they are the least well-trained in domestic matters of all three groups of women. By being chosen, or, rather, from their point of view, choosing to enter a permanent relationship at the beginning of their child-bearing period, they form a permanent relationship early and so do not have children from other men. Therefore, there are no "outside" children to be brought into the union.

By choosing women on the basis of their ability to satisfy their dominant need, the fishermen get women who do not already have children, while the cutters get women who do have young children. This process is the key to the creation of these household composition types and it demonstrates the indirect way a psychological need can influence the structure of an institution. Those qualities which draw the man to the woman have produced, in their own way, her possession of children by other men, or their absence. Therefore, in his choice of women the man determines the type of household he will set up. In other words, the man seeks neither the nuclear nor the complex household. He seeks the person, but this choice sets up his household.[9]

[9] This difference in life histories of the women in the two groups explains much of the general nature of the family, from the woman's point of view—since it is not enough to define mating patterns solely in terms of one partner's motivation. Women of the cane cutters have experienced events in their primary families which make them seek an impersonal role in which they can "take care" of the man. The fishermen's women are neither as trained nor need to base their relationship on the axis of care. They are capable of interpersonal relationships and actively seek a state in which these might be attained.

10

Summary, Conclusions, and Theory

I. THEORY

Before we may proceed to an integration of the ethnological and psychological materials, it is necessary to confront the most widely accepted opinion on the relationship between personality and culture. As we have seen earlier, the weight of contemporary theory maintains that cultural forms can be analyzed only in cultural terms, and the personality structure of individual members is therefore dependent upon the requirements of the cultural system. This argument might further insist that the relationship between cultural and psychological variables, discovered in the course of this study, establishes only a correlation between parallel conditions without isolating the significant causative factors.

In order to answer this theoretical position, and to demonstrate the possibility of establishing causal relationships, we must ask two questions. First, what institutional forces might have determined the specific structural features discovered in the economic and social units under study? Second, can the nature of the work groups, family organization and personality of the participating individuals be adequately explained by referring them back to either the larger economic units of which they are a part, or to a generalized West Indian culture pattern?

Our first line of reasoning is to recall that among comparable economic units in other West Indian areas, the work group organizations do not show a unitary structure. Because they have taken such vastly different forms, it is apparent that there is no fixed structure that exists wherever this economic organization is found. As the institution itself varies, we are then faced with the task of explaining its form. From this finding we may conclude that the estate or fishing organization, rather than being the primary determinant for most of the social or personality systems, becomes partially the dependent variable and the stimulus for a search into their origins.

In each case we have examined, the main factor to which variation may be attributed is the specific kind of gratification being sought by the men involved in that institution. These differences in personality are due to specific deprivation or gratification of basic needs during their childhood. Most important, these opportunities for satisfaction of psychological needs are related to conditions external to the institutional structure. In other words, the cause of the particular kind of psychological gratification is unrelated to the economic institution, as an institution. Therefore, it is incorrect to insist that personality is a residue of acquired motivations appropriate to the demands of the institution in which the individual must perform. It appears that personality development reaches a particular level and the institutions in which the individual is involved must adapt to meet these demands, just as they adapt to meet the demands of changing economic conditions.

It cannot be too heavily emphasized that the variables found responsible for the levels of personality, in each of these cases, lie outside the systematic organizational lines of the institution. Among the most important of these many factors are private ownership of land, residual cultural features (e.g., East Indian family structure), health, native residence and public welfare measures. In all of these, the key variable was found to be the opportunity for safety and love gratification. None of the above factors stands alone. There are stable families in those communities where there is the possibility for supplementary work on individually owned lands, and also where there is none—as in the East Indian communities studied by Jayawardena. It is equally true when neither possession of land nor lingering cultural patterns reinforce stability in the family, as with those of the fishermen of Dieppe Bay. In all cases, however, it is possible to identify a common element among these widely disparate variables: and that is the extent to which they have been able to satisfy basic psychological needs. Not only does the identification of a variety of factors unrelated to the larger institutions disprove the prevailing theoretical assumptions, but it is, moreover, evidence of the power of this approach that it enables the fieldworker to discover the common element. Therefore, we may conclude that both economic institutions permit a wide range of potential arrangement, within the context of the same overall organization. There are no necessary institutional requirements in these organizations determining work crew structure in any particular direction. An understanding of which forms will be instituted can only arise from knowledge of the specific psychological needs which the members are attempting to gratify.[1]

A further support for this point of view is found in the careers of the fishermen of Dieppe Bay. We have seen that, in terms of the dominant psychological characteristics of the population of St. Kitts, these men form a small atypical group. Although, originally, most of them worked on the neighboring estate in some capacity, their experiences in a structure organized to satisfy the dominant needs of most Kittitians were extremely frustrating. Because of this conflict between the type of economic organization they demand, and the one in which they found themselves working, they broke away and developed their economic life on a different basis. There are two salient points which bear upon this argument. First, if it is true that answers to cultural questions can only be found on the cultural level, and personality is produced by the overarching economic institution, why did these men find themselves so frustrated by the conditions of their work? If it is insisted that cultural forms develop the appropriate motivations in their participants necessary for the maintenance of the in-

[1] This discussion shows clearly the mechanisms of the proposed theoretical model. It is obvious that I am not maintaining a psychological reductionism or attempting to explain all aspects of culture in terms of basic needs. The value of the model is that it directs the investigator to a multitude of seemingly unrelated factors and enables him to trace out the causal network.

stitution, why did this basic conflict arise? Second, if this relationship between culture and personality is accurate, and it is argued that the fishermen, whose personality was supposedly formed to correspond with the plantation structure, merely left the estate for an alternative occupation, why did they then organize fishing on a basis radically different from that which exists on the estate? We have seen that it is possible to develop a fishing crew similar in most respects to the Kittitian cane gang. Why should the crew have been founded on a different basis?

A third line of reasoning helps answer the argument that what has been discovered is merely a correlation between isomorphic cultural and psychological processes. Recall that in recent years a change in the cutting gang has begun to develop. We have seen that gangs have begun to respond to tensions by splitting up into smaller units operating on a basis approximating the fishing crews and various estate structures in other West Indian areas. However, no event has occurred on the estate, in the last few years, that might have caused such a development. Instead, the significant economic changes that have occurred, such as mechanical packing and loading, would all help to argue that the estate's power over the workers has increased. What has been the case, though, is that workers born in the vicinity of the estate have begun to respond to recent changes such as improved sanitation, lowered infant and adult mortality, better housing, lessened exploitation and the creation of an arena for the redress of grievances—the union's activities. These have all served to provide increased gratifications of the workers' most basic needs, and the population has, therefore, been able to progress to higher levels of personality. Such changes in the workers' psychological states have enabled them to attempt to organize their work group structures on a different basis. These recent developments allow us to establish the causative relationship between the various factors we have been discussing, and furnish us with an example of the processes by which cultural and psychological factors interact over time to evolve the forms of culture.

One further word on the problem of isomorphism. If there were merely congruent structures on the psychological and cultural levels, it would be impossible to isolate widely dissimilar factors which result in varying examples of the same economic institution. However, we have seen that it is possible to identify the cause for the variation by examining the basic needs of the participants and their relationship to factors external to the estate system, as a system. As before, the fact that the agents responsible for the present level of personality lie outside the estate, together with the impetus coming from organismically based needs, demonstrates that this particular example of culture and personality is not merely an instance of viewing the same process from different vantage points. Parenthetically, it must be noted that an argument of isomorphism negates much of the culturological claim to explanation and leaves ambiguous the entire problem of determinants.

Now we must return to an examination of the general hypothesis I have proposed, and explore briefly the process by which these many factors have become integrated to form the organizations of personality and culture observed in Dieppe Bay.

II. THE INTEGRATION OF THE ENVIRONMENTAL, CULTURAL AND PSYCHOLOGICAL DETERMINANTS

In order to identify the determinants of the economic and social institutions of the two occupational groups, we must return to the theoretical model introduced in the first chapter. It has been proposed that cultural forms are the products of three antecedent variables; environment, historical sociocultural institutions and organismically based psychological needs. In this section, I shall first present the antecedent factors relevant to the culture of Dieppe Bay and then discuss the mechanisms by which they have been integrated to produce the contemporary village institutions.

The group of determinants which set the parameters within which the culture develops are the environmental features of the area. Of major importance to the establishment of a plantation system are the soil and rainfall conditions, which makes sugar cultivation both possible and profitable. Also of significance, on St. Kitts, is the great scarcity of land, which prevents the formation of a supplementary freehold land tenure system. The prerequisites for the development of a fishing industry are, in addition to the presence of an adequate supply of fish, the barrier reef and gently sloping beach area which permits boats to be launched and forms a safe harbor.

The second group of factors entering into the organizational process are the historical and contemporary sociocultural institutions impinging on St. Kitts. Of particular importance are the vicissitudes and mechanisms of the world market that receives the sugar; technological aspects of the industry, including sufficient capital to finance estates, industrial skills of both the managerial and industrial variety, appropriate machinery and the development of mechanization, and the concepts of economic organization brought to the island by the entrepreneurial class; English concepts of political and social organization, and value systems which serve as a model for lower-class aspiration; emancipation of the slaves forced upon the plantation society by pressures from England; and finally, the post-emancipation possibility for emigration.

The third set of determinants is the basic need structure universally present in all human beings. For the purposes of this study, it has been assumed that Maslow's personality theory is an accurate approximation and may be safely utilized. The two aspects of his work of immediate relevance are the specific needs on the various motivational levels and the concept of hierarchy—the principle of relationship between these needs, which affords the possibility of establishing variations in personality development not only from individual to individual, but from culture to culture.

These are the three independent determinants out of which the contemporary society is formed. Neither any one of these factors independently, nor any two in conjunction, can explain the specific institutional forms discovered in Dieppe Bay. The impetus from all three must be examined in order to account for the culture observed.

From the first two groups of determinants emerged

a set of conditions within which the population of St. Kitts was placed. The scarcity of land forced the majority of villages to be built along the side of the dank, unhealthy ravines. As I have noted earlier, only in the past few years has the government begun to establish villages on the more healthy arable land. Moreover, it has produced a residential pattern of small, closely packed houses in which a great many people reside. In his article "Psychological Effects of Housing on Growing Children," Winkel (1961) points out that the unavoidable noise produced by large numbers of people in the typical West Indian house constantly disturbs the sleeping baby. The baby's mother attempts to calm it by offering her breast, but as the baby is not hungry this fails to allay its crying. She then gets frustrated and starts to view the baby as a nuisance, thereby creating a spiral process in which the baby is looked after less and less. Furthermore, the crowded nature of the small house forces the child to upset things and get in the way. Therefore, to preserve the adults' possessions, he will be forbidden to touch things and will be continually scolded. "Thus they feel, and indeed often are, rejected, because they do not behave" (Winkel, 1961, p. 73).

The seasonal nature of employment determined by the work requirements of the estate, and the relatively low level of income, results in a meagre diet heavily emphasizing starchy foods. The lack of protein in the Kittitian diet is compounded by the inadequate pasturage available to the villagers on which to raise the animals, such as cows, goats, sheep or pigs, which might furnish a more balanced diet. The poor diet, coupled with the bad sanitary conditions, leads to an extremely high incidence of gastrointestinal diseases. Although the major diseases, such as malaria, have been virtually eradicated, the medical facilities available to the rural population are unfortunately inadequate to cope with what would ordinarily be a manageable form of illness. Therefore, both the infant mortality and adult death rates are very high; and this establishes a major condition of life on St. Kitts.

Another significant result of these economic determinants is the impossibility, for the majority of the population, to establish some measure of control over their own lives. We have seen that in other West Indian areas laborers may own their house plots as well as significant amounts of agricultural land. On St. Kitts, the population is forced to work solely on the estates and reside on estate-owned lands. Their entire lives, therefore, must be organized within the scope of the estate system.

The one major alternative to this pattern of life, of course, is emigration. We have seen in earlier chapters the magnitude of this response to life on St. Kitts, and some of its effects on the childhood experiences of the remaining members of the family. There are few Kittitians who have not been subject to its influence. Recall that during the period when these men were growing up, there were two adult women on St. Kitts for every man. Contemporaneously, in a period when the degree of movement appears lessened, in a village neighboring Dieppe Bay over thirty percent of the children are not being reared by their mothers.

Another aspect of West Indian population movement is the immigration of men to St. Kitts seeking jobs in the sugar industry. Compared to certain other islands, such as Nevis and Anguilla, St. Kitts offers opportunities for advancement lacking on their home islands. This attraction of St. Kitts is a function of its environmental conditions, and sets up, as we have seen, psychological conditions of great relevance to its economic institutions.

These medical, residential, nutritional, demographic, and economic conditions, which result from the environmental and past sociocultural institutions, lead to great instability of family life and an orientation of insecurity and exploitation in the adult world in general. The individual, growing up under these conditions, finds little gratification for his most basic needs. Viewing the population as a whole, there has been great deprivation of safety needs, and their dominant concern is, therefore, to find satisfaction of these deprived needs.

It is in this way that the basic human need structure becomes an antecedent determinant of culture. For the needs outlined by Maslow, events on the social level can serve to deprive pre-existing biological desires, but they do not create motivation. The most basic need deprived becomes a motivational force demanding a form of organization that will allow for a measure of gratification. It becomes the most important source of psychological energy available, while the needs higher on the hierarchy do not emerge, and are, therefore, irrelevant to the organization of culture.

As an antecedent determinant, the deprived need sets up a demand for safety gratifications which enters into a process of adjustment with the institutional demands. Because most of the population has little recourse but to work on the sugar estates, their predominant motivational orientation has caused them to structure their economic work groups in such a way as to receive as much gratification of the deprived needs as is possible. This readjustment process I have termed "reciprocal interchange." I conceive it to be a series of rearrangements over a period of time, perhaps similar to a bargaining process, until a balance is reached between the demands of the social and psychological systems. It is due to this process that the cane-cutting gang, which has been the object of study on the estate, has taken its specific form.

From the viewpoint of institutional analysis many other arrangements could have been made, as we have seen in Chapter 6. Neither estate structure, as such, environmental conditions or historical processes reveals why the large gang with its particular status and role configurations has evolved. It is only when we focus on the effect of the conditions of life on the individual and his response to them, in terms of his demands for basic need gratification, that we complete our understanding of the origins of cultural forms.

One great source of explanatory power achieved by including a psychological approach along with the more usual economic and cultural investigations, lies in the relationship that exists between the various basic needs. Human motivation is often dismissed from cultural explanation on the grounds that while all human beings are basically the same, there is an enormous variation among cultures: an object that varies cannot be explained by an object that is constant (White, 1949). However, if we recognize the patterning to be found among basic needs, it is evident that motivation is not a unitary force, either satisfied or deprived. Rather, the impetus that springs from the individual's participating in a culture exerts its force according to the demands of its most relevant need. In this way, personality gives both the direction and sets the limitations on the forms of culture.[2]

The influence of the level reached on the motivational hierarchy has been seen in the contrast with the fishing subculture of Dieppe Bay. The fishermen, as a group, have experienced far more safety gratification than the cutters. In particular, their experiences with disease and migration, which create an unstable family, were much less severe. These factors provided for increased safety gratifications, which, therefore, released energies higher on the motivational hierarchy. Specifically, the need structure of the fishermen is dominated by the love and self-esteem needs. As an atypical group of men, psychologically speaking, they retreated from the institutional structure related to the dominant cane cutters' needs. The occupational form of the fishing crew, as they have determined it, is neither higher nor lower than their own motivational level. They have taken the ecological givens—the market, the supply of fish, the distribution of fish over the sea, the harbor—and have adapted their economic structure to include an appropriate mechanism for gratifying their own needs. We have also seen, in Chapter 8, that the fishing crew could have been created on a basis similar to the cutting gang, or even according to a more integrated principle than it has. The difference between the two groups in Dieppe Bay is a clear indication of the ability of phase-specific needs to structure the cultural material with which they are presented.

In conclusion, I wish to emphasize my belief that, today, in psychology as well as in anthropology, we rely far too heavily on the influences of socially-conditioned learning to account for the dynamics of personality. In so doing, we lose sight of the qualitative meaning of

[2] We have seen a test of this hierarchical principle in the different responses of the two groups to deprivation of self-esteem. Although there have been equal degrees of deprivation, for the cutters it was an irrelevent experience and produced no effect on their personality. However, for the fishermen this has become an area of concern through the gratification of their love and belongingness needs, and they have responded to this specific deprivation by extreme demands for self-esteem gratifications.

psychological gratification, as well as the force exerted on the social order by these organismically-based demands. I have hoped, in the course of this study, to demonstrate that an investigation, which includes a study of psychological needs along with environmental and socio-economic variables, as basic determinants, greatly expands the social scientist's power to trace out the causal network of social phenomena.

APPENDIX I

Male Interview

House # _____ Date ____ Place of Interview_____
Subject's Name: _____ Age: _____ Occupation: _____ Marital State: _____

I. *Household Composition*

				Pl of		Arrival
1. Name	Age	Sex	Rel to S.	Birth	Occupation	in DB

_____
_____
_____
_____

2. Absent children of S and mate:
   Name   Age   Sex   Residence   Occupation

_____
_____
_____

II. *Occupation:*

1. Do you do other work along with your main job
_____
2. What type of work do you do in the dull season
_____
3. Did you ever work outside of St. Kitts ____ where
   _____ when _____ What sort of work
_____
4. Do you work any land _____ where _____ how
   much _____ crop _____
5. When did you start this type of work _____
6. What did you do before that _____
7. Did you ever work steadily at a different job _____

8. What work did your father do _____

9. Did your mother work regularly at a job _____

(fishermen only)

10. Is anyone in your family a fisherman?
    Name   Relation
    _____
    _____

11. Who taught you to fish _____ relationship __
    _____ when _____

12. Why did you choose fishing _____
    _____

13. What makes the men in the crew respect a particular
    fisherman _____

14. What is the captain responsible for _____

15. What is each crewman responsible for _____

16. What happens if the crewmen don't agree with the
    captain _____

17. What happens if the captain doesn't agree with the
    crew _____

18. What would make a crewman leave that crew ____
    _____

19. Do you prefer cane cutting or fishing? Why _____
    _____
    _____

20. Would you ever get together with another fisherman
    to buy a boat or a net? Why _____
    _____

21. How do you save money to buy pots _____
    _____

(cane cutters only)

22. Is anyone in your family a cane cutter?
    Name   Relation
    _____
    _____

23. When did you first start to work in the cane ____
    ____ age ____

24. What jobs did you do first _____

25. Why did you choose cutting _____

26. Would you want to be a head cutter? Why _____
_____

27. What makes the other men in the gang respect you
_____

28. What is the head cutter responsible for _____
_____

29. Are there ever arguments between him and the cutters? Over what _____

30. Do the men ever refuse to do what the head cutter
tells them? What things _____

31. If you decide not to work a day, do you tell the rest
of the gang? _____

32. How many men must show up for work to go on
_____ Why is that _____

33. Do you prefer fishing or cane cutting? Why _____
_____

III. *House*

1. Is your house owned ____ rented ____ owner _____
_____

2. Is your house plot owned ____ rented ____ owner
_____

3. Number of rooms in house _____

4. Electricity ____ radio ____ latrine ____ No. of beds
_____ Paint _____

5. Is there a fence around house _____

6. Do you have stock: chickens ____ pig ____ cow ____
goat ____ other _____

7. Do you have a bad dog _____

IV. *Personal Data*

1. Did you live with your mother at least till the age
of 5 years? _____ If not, how old were you when she
left _____

2. Who was in charge of you then _____ relationship _____ Did you live with your mother past the age of 5 _____ Until when _____

3. Did you live with your father at least till the age of 5 years _____ If not, how old were you when he left _____ Did you then have a father-in-law _____

4. Did you live with him past the age of 5 _____ until when _____

5. How many brothers and sisters did you have _____ how many died _____

6. Is your mother or father or the person who took care of you as a child alive _____ who _____ where _____

7. Do you support any person not in residence
　　　　Name　　　　　　Relationship

　　_____
　　_____
　　_____

8. What functions do you take part in _____
　　_____

9. Which church were you confirmed in _____

10. Are you a financial member _____

11. Were you ever a financial member of the union _____ Do you belong now _____ financial member _____

12. What do you do when you are not working _____
　　_____

13. What do you enjoy doing most _____
　　_____

V. Synergy

1. How long have you and your wife been living together _____

2. How much would you say that you and your wife resemble each other? That is, in terms of temperament and in those things which you feel are important in life? _____

3. In what ways are you different _____
　　_____

4. What things do you do together?
   rearing children _____
   sharing friends _____
   saving money _____
   owning stock _____
   looking after stock _____
   decision to live in DB _____
   eat together _____
   cook together _____
   work together _____
   go to town together _____
   outings together _____
   visiting together _____
   going to doctor together _____

5. What things do you own together _____
   _____

6. What things do you own separately?
       Man   *Woman*

   _____
   _____
   _____
   _____
   _____
   _____

APPENDIX II

Female Interview

Date _____ Place of Interview _____
1. Name _____ Man _____ Age __
2. Place of birth _____ Arrival in DB _____
3. Residence before DB _____ Dates _____
   Before that _____
4. Why did you come to DB _____
5. Religion _____ Financial _____ Attendance _____
6. Do you take part in any functions _____
7. What standard did you complete in school _____
8. Do you own the house _____ date purchased _____
9. Do you have family in DB? Relations: _____
10. How long did you live with your mother _____
    Then who looked after you _____ rel. _____ how
    long _____ Was your mother still in the village ___
    island _____
11. How long did you live with your father _____
    Did you have a father-in-law _____ how long _____
    Was your father still in the village _____ island _____
12. How many older brothers _____ yb _____ older
    sisters _____ ys _____ How many died when you
    were a child _____
13. Who would you say was good to you as a child
    Name_____ rel _____ at what ages _____
    _____   _____   _____
    _____   _____   _____
14. Were any of your brothers cane cutters or fishermen
    _____

228

15. What kind of work did your father do _____

16. What kind of work did your mother do _____

17. How many children do you have (including dead and miscarried)

a) with S
    name   *age*   *sex*   *residence*
    _____
    _____
    _____
    _____

b) with another man
    name   age   sex   residence   # yrs with S   caretaker
    _____
    _____

18. Did you ever live with another man _____
    Name   dates   occupation   older or younger
    _____
    _____

19. Did any of the above children live there with you
    _____

        Name   *dates*
    _____
    _____

20. Marital state _____ How many years have you
    and S been living together _____

21. When did you and S get married _____

22. Were your parents married _____

23. Do you do any work _____
    _____

24. Did you ever work _____ when did you stop _____
    why _____

            (fisherman's woman)

25. Do you sell fish _____ how often _____

26. Do you sell most of his fish _____

27. Do you sell most in the village or out _____

28. Do you have steady customers _____ how many _____
    monthly _____ weekly _____

29. Do you sell more of his fish in the gar or pot fishing time _____

(cutter's woman)

30. Who do you get your fish from _____

31. Do you have trouble getting fish _____

32. What is the best relish to give a family _____

(all)

33. How much relish do you buy each week
    December-February   *March-July*   *August-November*
    $_____ $_____ $_____

34. How much do you spend at the shop each week
    December-February   *March-July*   *August-November*
    $_____ $_____ $_____

35. What is a father supposed to do for the children
    _____

36. What is a mother supposed to do for the children
    _____

37. When you are doing your home domestic work, do friends sometimes help you or keep you company or talk to you while you do the work _____
    _____

38. Would you rather have boy or girl babies _____

39. Does S need a lot of looking after _____

40. What are the good things about S _____

41. What does he like best about you _____

42. Do you and S have some fights. About what _____
    _____

43. What would you say are the best things about men
    _____

44. What would you say are the worst things about men
    _____

45. What would be the nicest thing that could happen to you _____
    _____

46. What would be the worst thing that could happen to you _____

_____

47. What would you say is the difference between marriage and common law _____

_____

APPENDIX III

Name: _____ Date: _____ Time: _____
Place of Interview: _____

1. Money is
2. Food
3. I am proud of
4. A friend
5. A father
6. I feel happy when
7. A mother
8. When I was a child
9. My biggest worry
10. A family
11. I get vexed when
12. People from other islands who come here
13. A wife
14. When someone dies I
15. I am sad because I
16. I love
17. When men curse
18. Women
19. I want
20. A grandmother
21. I am good at
22. When they tell me I can't do it I

23. When I am not treated right
24. A sister
25. (A Head Cutter—A Captain)
26. Men
27. Most girls
28. The people around here
29. A woman older than me
30. Responsibility
31. A brother
32. Hit
33. A woman younger than me

Projective Questions

1. If you were given $2,000, what would you do with it?
2. What kind of friend would you choose?
3. What should be done with people who ride bicycles carelessly?
4. What should be done with children who steal things?
5. What is the worst thing that could happen to you?
6. What is the nicest thing that could happen to you?
7. If a magic man could make you into a child again, what would you like to do most?
8. What did you miss most as a child?
9. What happens if the man over you doesn't treat you right?
10. What is the worst thing about women?
11. What is the best thing about women?
12. What should be done with people from another island who do rudeness?
13. And if he were from Dieppe Bay?

Bibliography

ADLER, A. *The Individual Psychology of Alfred Adler*. Ansbacher, H. L. and Ansbacher, R. R. (eds.) New York: Basic Books, 1956.

ANGYAL, A. *Foundations for a Science of Personality*. Cambridge, Mass.: Harvard Unixersity Press, 1958.

ARONOFF, M. "Middle Mass Voluntary Associations in a West Indian Village." Unpublished ms., 1962.

ARONOFF, M., MELEMED, B., and RAYMOND, N. "Report of the Second Brandeis University Caribbean Expedition, St. Kitts—Summer, 1961." Unpublished ms., 1962.

ATKINSON, J. W., (ed.) *Motives in Fantasy, Action, and Society*. Princeton, New Jersey: D. Van Nostrand, 1958.

ATKINSON, J. W. and McCLELLAND, D. C. "The Effect of Different Intensities of the Hunger Drive on Thematic Apperception." In Atkinson, J. W., (ed.), *Motives in Fantasy, Action, and Society*. Princeton, New Jersey: D. Van Nostrand, 1958.

BLAKE, J. *Family Structure in Jamaica*. Glencoe, Illinois: The Free Press of Glencoe, 1961.

CLARKE, E. *My Mother Who Fathered Me*. London: George Allen and Unwin, Ltd., 1957.

DAVENPORT, W. "A Comparative Study of Two Jamaican Fishing Villages." Unpublished Ph.D. dissertation, Yale University, 1956.

DOOB, L. W. *Becoming More Civilized*. New Haven: Yale University Press, 1960.

FREILICH, M. "Cultural Diversity Among Trinidadian Peasants." Unpublished Ph.D. dissertation, Columbia University, 1960.

FREUD, S. "Totem and Taboo." In *The Basic Writings of Sigmund Freud*, New York: The Modern Library, 1938.

GOLDSTEIN, K. *The Organism*. New York: American Book Company, 1939.

HANDLER, J. "Land Exploitatative Activities and Economic Patterns in a Barbados Village." Unpublished Ph.D. dissertation, Brandeis University, 1965.

HAY, D. R. *Agricultural Land Use of Guadeloupe*. Washington,

234

D.C., National Academy of Sciences. National Research Council. 1961.

HEYNS, R. W., et al. "A Scoring Manual for the Affiliation Motive," in Atkinson, J. W., (ed.), Motives in Fantasy, Action, and Society. Princeton: D. Van Nostrand, 1958.

JAYAWARDENA, C. Conflict and Solidarity in a Guianese Plantation. London: The Athlone Press, University of London, 1963.

KARDINER, A. The Individual and his Society. New York: Columbia University Press, 1939.

KLASS, M. "Cultural Persistence in a Trinidad East Indian Community." Unpublished Ph.D dissertation, Columbia University, 1959.

KLUCKHOHN, C. and MURRAY, H. A. "Personality Formation: the Determinants," in Kluckhohn, C. and Murray, H. A. (eds.), Personality in Nature, Society, and Culture. (2nd ed.) New York: Alfred Knopf, 1956.

KUCZYNSKI, R. R. A Demographic Survey of the British Colonial Empire. Vol. III. Oxford University Press, 1953.

LEE, D. Freedom and Culture. New York, Prentice-Hall, Inc., 1959.

McDOUGALL, W. An Introduction to Social Psychology. London: Methuen & Co., Ltd., 1960.

MALINOWSKI, B. A Scientific Theory of Culture and Other Essays. New York: Oxford University Press, 1960.

MASLOW, A. H. Motivation and Personality. New York: Harper & Brothers, 1954.

MERRILL, G. C. The Historical Geography of St. Kitts and Nevis, The West Indies. Mexico: Instituto Panamericano De Geografia E. Historia, 1958.

MINTZ, S. W. "Canamelar." In Steward, J. H. (ed.), The Peoples of Puerto Rico. Urbana: University of Illinois Press, 1956.

MINTZ, S. W. "The Employment of Capital by Market Women in Haiti." In Firth, R. and Yamey, B. S. (eds.), Capital, Saving and Credit in Peasant Societies. Chicago: Aldine Publishing Company, 1964.

PARSONS, T. and SHILS, E. A. (eds.), Toward a General Theory of Action. Cambridge, Mass.: Harvard University Press, 1962.

PROUDFOOT, M. J. Population Movements in the Caribbean. Report of the Caribbean Commission. Port of Spain: Trinidad, 1950.

Report of a Commission of Inquiry into the Sugar Industry of British Guiana. Colonial Office. London, 1949.

ROHEIM, G. "The Origin and Function of Culture." New

York: Nervous and Mental Disease Monographs, No. 69, 1943.

RUBIN, V. *Trinidad Youth Study.* Research Institute for the Study of Man. Unpublished, 1957.

SHIPLEY, T. E. and VEROFF, J. "A Projective Measure of the Need for Affiliation," in Atkinson, J. W. (ed.) *Motives in Fantasy, Action, and Society.* Princeton, New Jersey: D. Van Nostrand, 1958.

SMITH, M. G. *West Indian Family Structure.* Seattle: University of Washington Press. 1962.

SMITH, R. T. "Community Status and Family Structure in British Guiana." In Bell, N. W., and Vogel, E. F. (eds.), *The Family.* The Free Press of Glencoe, Illinois, 1960.

SOULBURY, P. C. *The Organization of the Sugar Industry of St. Christopher.* Crown Agents for the Colonies. London, 1949.

SPIRO, M. E. "An Overview and a Suggested Reorientation," in F. L. K. Hsu (ed.), *Psychological Anthropology.* Homewood, Illinois: Dorsey Press, 1961.

STEWARD, J. H. *Theory of Culture Change.* Urbana, Illinois: University of Illinois Press, 1958.

WALLACE, A. F. C. "The New Culture and Personality," in Gladwin, T. and Sturtevant, W. C. (eds.), *Anthropology and Human Behavior.* Theo. Gans' Sons, Inc., Brooklyn, New York, 1962.

WHITE, L. A. *The Science of Culture.* New York: Grove Press, Inc., 1949.

WHITE, R. W. *Ego and Reality in Psychoanalytic Theory.* New York: International Universities Press, Inc., 1963.

WHITING, J. W. M., *et al.* "The Learning of Values," in Vogt, E. Z. and Albert, E. M., *The Peoples of Rimrock.* Cambridge: Harvard University Press. (In press.)

WHITING, J. W. M. "Socialization, Process and Personality," in F. L. K. Hsu (ed.), *Psychological Anthropology.* Homewood, Illinois: The Dorsey Press, Inc., 1961.

WINKEL, C M. "Psychological Effects of Housing on Growing Children," in Carter, Rev. S. E. (ed.), *The Adolescent in the Changing Caribbean.* Jamaica: University College of the West Indies. Jamaica, 1961.

General Index

Index of Names